Believing as BAPTISTS

Believing as Baptists

Rev. George T. Brooks Sr.

Townsend **Press**
Nashville, Tennessee

Unless otherwise noted, Scripture quotations are from the New American Standard Bible®. Copyright © 1960, 1962, 1963, 1968, 1971, 1972, 1973, 1975, 1977, 1995 by The Lockman Foundation. Used by permission. (www.Lockman.org)

Those marked KJV are from the King James Version of the Bible.

Copyright © 2016 by George Brooks Sr.
All rights reserved.

ISBN 978-1-939225-87-0

TABLE OF CONTENTS

Introduction _____ vii

Chapter 1
The Value of What We Believe _____ 1

Chapter 2
What We Believe about God _____ 4

Chapter 3
What We Believe about the Birth of Jesus _____ 8

Chapter 4
What We Believe about Jesus _____ 12

Chapter 5
What We Believe about the Holy Spirit _____ 18

Chapter 6
What We Believe about the Bible—Part 1 _____ 24

Chapter 7
What We Believe about the Bible—Part 2 _____ 27

Chapter 8
What We Believe about the Fall of Man _____ 31

Chapter 9
What We Believe about Salvation _____ 35

Chapter 10
What We Believe about the Eternal Security
of the Believer _____ 39

Chapter 11
What We Believe about the Church _____ 47

Chapter 12
    What We Believe about the Ordinances
    of the Church _____ 57

Chapter 13
    What We Believe about the Correct Day
    of Worship _____ 64

Chapter 14
    What We Believe about the Church and Its Mission _____ 69

Chapter 15
    What We Believe about the Work of the Holy Spirit
    in the Life of the Church _____ 73

INTRODUCTION

The Baptist church is facing some challenging times. One of the major reasons for the challenges of the day is the uncertainty that members of Baptist churches have about what they believe.

Members of Baptist churches have listened to so many people say that one church or religion is as good as another for so long that they have started to believe it. But it is important to understand that one church or religion is not as good as another if that church or religion is not rightly dividing God's Word.

In this series of lessons it is the intent of the writer to examine a few beliefs held by Baptist Christians. It is the writer's belief that a person can be Baptist and Christian at the same time without any dividing line.

It is not the writer's intent to examine all that Baptists believe, nor to even totally exhaust all that could be said on any beliefs covered in this series. This is merely an effort to give exposure to some of the things the writer feels to be of value in the life and work of the Baptist church.

All of these lessons should be studied with an open mind and an open Bible in order that God might challenge each reader to know what he or she believes as a Baptist. This growing understanding should result in the reader's not being ashamed of being a Baptist.

Many thanks go to my wife, Sarah, my daughter, Octavia, Sister Charlene Stuart, and Sister Carolyn Butler for their work in the preparation of the manuscript.

May God bless you on your journey into *Believing as Baptists*.

Chapter 1

THE VALUE OF WHAT WE BELIEVE
(1 Peter 3:15; 2 Peter 3:17)

There are people who feel that where religion is concerned, it does not matter what people believe as long as they are sincere in their beliefs. But it is possible to be sincere and yet be sincerely wrong.

It was because of what the early church believed that their lives were transformed, and they were instruments in the transformation of lives about them.

It is the church's business to help people understand and accept the basic beliefs of Christianity. There is an urgent need for people who believe and live the great truths of the Gospel and who know how to bear witness to the people around them.

People need to know that if they do not stand for something they will fall for anything. The church faces a great deal of spiritual ignorance and indifference in this day, simply because people feel that just any religion or church is as good as another.

People need to know and understand that what they believe has a bearing on personal, social, and world problems.

People never really undertake the Christian way of life in a strong and positive way if they do not know what is involved in it. You can never live any higher than you believe.

I. How to Bear Witness to What Is Believed

It was not unusual in Peter's day for Christians to be asked at any time to give an account of their faith. Sometimes they had to do so in courts of law before hostile government officials. Therefore, they needed to be well grounded in the fundamental truths of Christianity so that they could make a worthy defense of their hope.

The words of 1 Peter 3:15 indicate the manner in which Christians are to defend the hope: "Sanctify Christ as Lord in your hearts, always being ready to make a defense to everyone who asks you to give an account for the hope that is in you, yet with gentleness and reverence."

Beliefs are to be shared with meekness and godly fear. Doctrine does not exist primarily for the sake of argument. What is believed is the very thing that determines what people become and what they do. A false idea about God will lead to an unworthy attitude toward life. The reason for a good portion of poor Christian living is weak Christian beliefs.

The preparation for our being ready to defend our beliefs is for Jesus Christ to be set apart in the heart. He must reign and rule in the heart.

II. Right Beliefs and Salvation

When the beliefs are right, the Christian is given salvation, and has hope and stability. When salvation is experienced, one of the first things touched is a person's intellect. Paul said to the Thessalonians, "God has chosen you from the beginning for salvation through sanctification by the Spirit and faith in the truth" (2 Thessalonians 2:13b).

There is a body of revealed truth which the Christian accepts. The intellectual acceptance of the truth will not save anyone by itself. But this intellectual acceptance of the truth is basic to the faith that saves.

A second important thing in the experience of salvation is the emotions. Intellectual acceptance of the truth feeds the emotions, and then the emotions motivate the conduct. It is through truth accepted by the mind that the heart is prepared to accept the Gospel.

The third thing of importance in the experience of salvation is the volition or will. What is believed in the intellect feeds the emotions of the heart, and this causes the will to be moved.

III. The Danger of Instability (2 Peter 3:14-18)

Here in these verses Peter drew attention to the writings of Paul. It is very apparent that he regarded these writings as Scripture.

Peter said that there were some things in the writings of Paul that were hard to understand. These things the unlearned, the untaught, and the unstable distorted or twisted. The unlearned were not those who lacked schooling but those whose minds were untrained and undisciplined in habits of thought. The unstable were those whose habits of living were not well established.

People who are untrained in the Scriptures and unstable in their emotional and practical living are apt to twist the meaning of the Scriptures. Peter said that they do this to their own spiritual ruin.

It may not appear to be so, but doctrinal error is dangerous ground on which to stand. Peter said to his readers, "You . . . beloved . . . be on your guard so that you are not carried away by the error of unprincipled men and fall from your own steadfastness" (2 Peter 3:17).

Peter closed this chapter by giving his readers a very good piece of advice. Peter said, "Grow in the grace and knowledge of our Lord and Savior Jesus Christ" (2 Peter 3:18a).

The knowledge to which Peter made reference in this passage is more than head knowledge. It is knowledge that comes from close, committed living in loving fellowship with the Lord.

▶ FOR DISCUSSION

1. What makes it so important to know what one believes?

2. How should a Christian bear witness to Christian beliefs?

3. What effect(s) do beliefs have on salvation?

4. What effect(s) do wrong teachings have on a person's life?

Chapter 2

WHAT WE BELIEVE ABOUT GOD
(Isaiah 40:28-31)

In this age there are many false conceptions about God. There are those who view God as merely a policeman who protects them or who punishes them when they are wrong. There are others who picture God in terms of what they saw in their father and mother during childhood.

There are people who look upon God as a sort of old man, and therefore old-fashioned and out of touch with our contemporary issues. It seems that with many people their conception of God has not grown with modern needs. Their idea of God has become static while all else around them has progressed. Each new experience encountered in life gives God a chance to reveal Himself in a new and different way.

There are also people who see God as being so far away that He could not spare time to look after the needs of people.

There are even people who see God as a disappointment because He has not answered their prayers. The list of the various views about God could go on and on. What is believed about God is important because it affects all the other doctrines that people believe. It also commands love and loyalty.

I. The Form of God (John 4:23-24)

Here in this passage from John, Jesus is seen conversing with the Samaritan woman at Jacob's Well. Jesus said to her concerning God, "God is Spirit." These words describe God as not having a material or visible form. Yet, because He is a person, He can be worshipped in sincerity and honesty.

To suggest that God has no material or visible form is to suggest that He is not subject to the limitations to which the human body is subject. The Bible describes God as having feet, a heart, arms, a mouth, ears, and other body parts. But these words are used to describe how God functions.

Another important factor to consider is that God is not the Father of all people. He is the Creator of all people, but He is the Father of only those who have accepted Him as Savior and Lord. The apostle John wrote in his gospel, "But as many as received Him, to them He gave the right to become children of God, even to those who believe in His name" (John 1:12). Jesus even taught His disciples to pray, "Our Father."

II. The Attributes of God

It has been suggested that God has eleven attributes, seven of which are natural and four of which are moral. They will help in understanding the greatness and goodness of God.

   A. God's Natural Attributes
     1. Omnific, self-existent (Genesis 1:1; John 1:1)
     2. Omniscient (Psalm 139:1-6)
     3. Omnipresent (Psalm 139:7-12)
     4. Omnipotent (Matthew 17:20)
     5. Immutable (Malachi 3:6; Job 23:13)
     6. Immense (Exodus 13:21)
     7. Eternal (Deuteronomy 33:27)

   B. God's Moral Attributes
     1. Holiness (Isaiah 6:3)
     2. Righteousness (Deuteronomy 32:4)
     3. Truth (Hebrews 6:18)
     4. Love (1 John 4:16)

When consideration is given to the attributes of God, the resulting knowledge is that God is both transcendent and immanent. To say that God is transcendent is to say that God is above and beyond all His creation. He is in heaven on His throne, ruling the world. But to say that God is immanent is to say that He is near, even in the very air that humanity breathes.

III. God as Creator and Sustainer (Isaiah 40:27-31)

Here in this familiar passage from the book of Isaiah, the prophet was not addressing people who had no knowledge of God. The words were written to people whom God had blessed in a very special way, yet their hope had grown dim. They had come to the point of feeling that their God had forsaken them.

In verse 27, Isaiah noted that the people were saying that God no longer had any interest in them. In order to contradict this false idea about God, Isaiah wrote this passage of Scripture—where he said the following:

> Do you not know? Have you not heard? The everlasting God, the LORD, the Creator of the ends of the earth Does not become weary or tired. His understanding is inscrutable. He gives strength to the weary, And to him who lacks might He increases power. Though youths grow weary and tired, and vigorous young men stumble badly, Yet those who wait for the LORD Will gain new strength; . . . They will run and not get tired, They will walk and not become weary." (Isaiah 40:28-31)

Notice how Isaiah described God. Isaiah saw God as the following:

A. Everlasting—This shows God's endurance.

B. The Lord—God is master; His authority is absolute.

C. The Creator—All things find their origin in God.

D. Unfainting and Unwearied—This shows God's inexhaustible strength. Because His strength is inexhaustible, he "gives strength to the weary and to him who lacks might he increases power." This is a picture of God's pity and power. The strong are strong by the power of God, and the tired and weary are also made strong by the same power.

God is interested in the needs of man. When we wait on Him, God makes us like Himself, that is, unfainting and unwearied.

E. **Unsearchable in His Understanding**—God knows all things, large and small. God knows the strong and the weak alike.

When Israel thought about God as Creator, they called Him *Elohim*. This name means "strong one."

When Israel thought about God's power to redeem, they referred to Him by the name *Jehovah*.

When Israel considered God as their master, they called Him *Adonai*.

When Israel looked upon God as the Almighty, they called Him *El Shaddai* (see Genesis 17:1).

When God provided Abraham with a ram on Mount Moriah to sacrifice instead of his son, Abraham called that place *Jehovah Jireh* (see Genesis 22:1-14). This meant that "God will provide."

After Israel had defeated the Amalekites, Moses erected an altar and called it *Jehovah Nissi* (see Exodus 17:15). This title means "God is my banner."

When God gave Israel peace in the midst of her storms, they called Him *Jehovah Shalom* (see Judges 6:24).

If by chance all these names and titles cannot be remembered, just call God God.

▶ FOR DISCUSSION

1. What are some of the modern beliefs about God?

2. What is the form of God?

3. What are the attributes of God?

4. What are some of the names by which God has been called?

Chapter 3

WHAT WE BELIEVE ABOUT THE BIRTH OF JESUS
(Luke 2:10-11)

The story of the birth of Jesus is a story that never grows old. It is as beautiful and interesting as it was the night it was told to the shepherds who were the first to receive the announcement of His birth.

The angel said to the shepherds, "I bring you good news of great joy which will be for all the people" (Luke 2:10).

"Good news of a great joy" is a characteristic of the Gospel. Since this is true, being a Christian always holds the potential for having joy. This joy is not something that comes automatically. Neither is it forced. It is dependent upon the heart's response to Christ.

If God had not sent Jesus into the world to give His life, this world would be a joyless place. Because of what God did in Jesus Christ, the power of sin has been broken, eternal life has been made a possibility, and the saved have a sure inheritance in the kingdom of heaven.

The world is filled with pain, sorrow, and wickedness. Most people are involved either in a sad struggle for existence or a mad struggle for power and pleasure.

Many people are searching for answers to problems, but many times the answers multiply the problems. But the Christian is intended to be on a different level, because he or she knows that in Jesus Christ there is help and hope.

I. A Revelation of God as a Living Person

Here in this background Scripture an angel of the Lord is seen announcing to shepherds the Good News of the birth of Jesus. The birth of Jesus revealed God as a living person and the Savior of humankind. Isaiah prophesied concerning Jesus, "The Lord Himself will give you a sign: Behold, a virgin will be with child and bear a son, and she will call His name Immanuel" (Isaiah 7:14).

When the angel of the Lord told Joseph of this prophecy, he said that the interpretation of the word "Immanuel" is "God with us" (see Matthew 1:23).

Not only did God perform a great work in creating the world, but He also performed an even greater work in redeeming it through Jesus Christ. Jesus' being born is God's gift of Himself for the sake of the world.

The birth of Jesus is so amazing that it is often treated almost as a myth. People sometimes fail to feel the importance of it. The miracle of the birth of Jesus is not seen by many people as an event that meant hope for fallen humanity. But without Jesus' coming into the world, God would have never been revealed as a living Person.

II. A Revelation of God's Love for Humanity

The birth of Jesus meant that God had not given up on a sinful race. He had used Abraham to help prepare the world for salvation. God had used other patriarchs to help prepare the world for salvation. He had even used the Law and the Prophets, but none of those things or persons was successful. In Jesus Christ, God provided redemption for humanity through His own self-giving.

The heart of the message that was brought to the shepherds was that a Savior was born. The emphasis was not on the fact that a baby was born. Babies had been born too many times to count. This was the first time a Savior had been born.

The apostle John said, "We have seen and testify that the Father has sent the Son to be the Savior of the world" (1 John 4:14). The hope of humanity lay in Jesus' being the Savior. Jesus was born a Savior, He died a Savior, and He lives evermore as the Savior.

Other religions have their prophets and teachers, but Christianity is the only religion that has a Savior. Other religions take men as they are and leave them as they find them, but Jesus came to make men new. Paul said, "If anyone is in Christ, he is a new creature; the old things passed away; behold, new things have come" (2 Corinthians 5:17).

The coming of Jesus was the greatest compliment ever paid to the human race, for it said that God cares about humanity.

III. A Revelation of a New Life for Humankind

Because of Jesus Christ Christians now know what they did not know. As the Son of God, Jesus has given humanity an understanding of God never known before. Jesus said, "He who has seen Me has seen the Father" (John 14:9b).

Because of Jesus Christ, not only do Christians know what they did not know—they also can become what they have not been. The apostle John said, "As many as received Him, to them He gave the right to become children of God" (John 1:12). Jesus Christ came into the world on a mission of regeneration.

There is no other power in this world that can make people children of God but that which is found in Jesus Christ. The only thing that limits the operation of the power of Jesus in this life is people's rejection of Jesus.

Jesus came to transform natural weaklings into spiritual giants. He came to transform slaves to sin into servants of the Most High God. Jesus came to give victory for defeat, joy for sorrow, and salvation for damnation.

Because of Jesus Christ, people can have hope at the very place where they lost heart. It is important to understand that hope does not come easily. The birth of Jesus is a reminder that life has a new beginning in Jesus Christ.

Because of Jesus Christ, those who believe can now belong where they have never been able to belong before. There are so many things that separate people from one another in this world. But Jesus Christ brings people together and gives them a sense of belonging.

A person may not have any other family on this earth, but he or she can praise God that he or she is a member of the royal family of God.

FOR DISCUSSION

1. What did the birth of Jesus reveal about God?
2. What did the birth of Jesus reveal about humanity?

Chapter 4

WHAT WE BELIEVE ABOUT JESUS
(John 1:1, 14; Matthew 16:13-17)

One day near the end of the earthly ministry of Jesus, He asked the Pharisees a question: "What do you think about the Christ, whose son is He?" (Matthew 22:42a). That question was very appropriate at that time, and it remains relevant today.

In spite of some people's having very shallow beliefs about Jesus, please be assured that it does make a difference what a person thinks about Him. What is believed about Jesus determines the relationship a person has with Him, and that relationship determines a person's destiny.

In this lesson, attention shall be focused on the nature and person of Jesus. His nature and person set forth His relationship to God and humanity.

I. The Origin of Jesus

Many people believe that Jesus became the Son of God the night He was born in Bethlehem. But Jesus is the eternal Son of God. Just as God the Father is eternal and self-existing, the same thing holds true about Jesus.

When God said, "Let Us make man in Our image, according to Our likeness" (Genesis 1:26a), Jesus was included in the "Us" and the "Our."

When God raised the question in the presence of Isaiah, "Whom shall I send, and who will go for Us?" (Isaiah 6:8), Jesus was included in the "Us."

The gospel of Matthew traced the origin of Jesus back to Abraham. The gospel of Luke traced the origin of Jesus back to

Adam, and the gospel of John traced the origin of Jesus back to God Himself.

Bethlehem was not the first home of Jesus. John said, "In the beginning was the Word, and the Word was with God, and the Word was God" (John 1:1). In this one verse, John affirmed the eternity, the personality, and the deity of Jesus. He is as ageless as God; He is God; and being God, He is deity.

In the original Greek text, this verse is deeper than the mind can conceive. The tense of the verb "was" is the imperfect tense. This does not have reference to the past; it rather suggests that something is continuous. Jesus has always been a continuous entity. Jesus has been described as an eternal contemporary. He has been here before and during every age in history.

Jesus also said to the Jews, "Truly, truly, I say to you, before Abraham was born, I am" (John 8:58). The phrase "I am" is also a sacred name of God (see Exodus 3:14-15). This name was used by God of Himself as He spoke to Moses on the back side of Mount Horeb.

The apostle John also said, "And the Word became flesh, and dwelt among us, and we saw His glory, glory as of the only begotten from the Father, full of grace and truth" (John 1:14).

This verse declares the incarnation of Jesus. The incarnation of Jesus made Him the God-man. He became fully man while remaining fully God. In Jesus Christ, God does not merely dwell among men; He has joined Himself unto men. The Word did not merely dwell in flesh; John said that the Word became flesh.

As John looked upon Jesus as the God-man, he was fascinated by what he saw. He saw Jesus as being full of grace and truth. Jesus did not come into the world to tell humanity about grace; He came to bring grace.

Others who had come on the scene before Jesus and those who have come since Jesus only teach and preach the truth, but Jesus is the Truth. Jesus said of Himself, "I am the way, and the truth, and the life; no one comes to the Father but through Me" (John 14:6).

Jesus displayed the grace of God by living among humanity for thirty-three years.

Jesus displayed the grace of God by giving His life for the sins of the world.

Jesus displayed the grace of God by getting up from the grave in order to justify and pardon the guilty.

II. The Earthly Life of Jesus
A. *His Birth*

Jesus was born around 4 or 5 BC of a virgin named Mary. Jesus did not have an earthly father. The Virgin Birth was God's method of breaking the laws of heredity. The birth of Jesus proves that God is not subject to any human or physical limitations.

It was so majestic that it was proclaimed by an angel from the Lord and a heavenly host praised God by saying, "Glory to God in the highest, and on earth peace among men with whom He is pleased" (Luke 2:14b).

B. *His Character*

Jesus had a sinless character. The apostle Peter described Jesus as having no sin or any deceit in His mouth (see 1 Peter 2:22).

The writer of the book of Hebrews said about Jesus, "For we do not have a high priest who cannot sympathize with our weaknesses, but One who has been tempted in all things as we are, yet without sin" (Hebrews 4:15).

All sin separates from God; but Jesus maintained unbroken fellowship with the Father because He committed no sin. There has to be agreement with what Pilate said about Jesus, "I find no fault in Him" (John 19:6b, KJV).

C. *His Personal Claims*

1. *Jesus Claimed to Be God.*

Near the end of the earthly ministry of Jesus He said to Philip, "He who has seen Me has seen the Father" (John 14:9b). Jesus also claimed, "I and the Father are one" (John 10:30).

2. **Jesus Claimed to Be God by Claiming to Be Able to Forgive Sins.**
One day while Jesus was preaching in Capernaum, a man was let down into His presence through the roof of the house where Jesus was preaching. Jesus said to the man, "Son, your sins are forgiven" (Mark 2:5).

As soon as Jesus made the claim of forgiving the man of his sins, the Pharisees began to murmur. They said, "Who can forgive sins but God alone?" (Mark 2:7b). For once, these Pharisees were right. No one can forgive sin except God, and Jesus forgives sins. That therefore proves Him to be God.

3. **Jesus Claimed to Deserve First Place in the Lives of Believers.**
Jesus claimed to merit first place in the lives of men. Jesus told His followers that if they wished to follow Him they must deny themselves (see Matthew 16:24). Those who wish to follow Jesus must forsake all and love Him above all.

No mere man can lay claim to all of man's loyalty. Only God can do that; therefore, Jesus is God.

4. **Jesus Claimed to Judge the World.**
Jesus claimed to be the judge of the world. Jesus said to a group of Jews, "For not even the Father judges anyone, but He has given all judgment to the Son, in order that all honor the Son even as they honor the Father. He who does not honor the Son does not honor the Father who sent Him" (John 5:22-23, NASB).

God has three powerful functions: that of Creator, that of Preserver, and that of Judge; and Jesus is the agent of all three.

III. Jesus as the Son of the Living God (Matthew 16:13-17)

Here in this background Scripture, Jesus had come to a crisis in His ministry. He had called His disciples to Himself and withdrawn from Galilee into the regions around Caesarea Philippi. This happened about six months before the crucifixion of Jesus.

His disciples had walked in close fellowship with Him for three years now. The hour had arrived for Jesus to test their faith. He wanted to know just exactly what they believed about Him.

Jesus began by asking His disciples what the common opinions were about Him. Jesus said, "Who do people say that the Son of Man is?" (Matthew 16:13b).

The answers that were given to this question were very complimentary. Some people were saying that Jesus was John the Baptist; others were saying that He was Elijah. There was also a group that was saying that Jesus was Jeremiah. Then there was another group that did not know how to describe Jesus, but they did associate Him with one of the prophets.

Jesus left the common opinion of the people and turned the force of His next question directly on His disciples. Jesus asked them, "But who do you say that I am?" (Matthew 16:15).

Peter answered the question raised by Jesus for both himself and the other disciples. Peter said, "You are the Christ, the Son of the living God" (Matthew 16:16). With this answer Peter struck a very high note because he was saying more than he realized he was saying.

As the Christ, Jesus was the chosen one of God. As the disciples walked with Jesus day after day, they watched Him do many things that proved to them that He was more than just a man.

Jesus assured Peter that the answer he had given did not begin with Himself or any other human. Jesus said to Peter, "Flesh and blood did not reveal this to you, but My Father who is in heaven" (Matthew 16:17).

IV. Why Jesus Came into the World
A. *Jesus Came into the World to Reveal God.*
The apostle John said about Jesus' coming into the world, "No one has seen God at any time; the only begotten God who is in the bosom of the Father, He has explained Him" (John 1:18).

B. **_Jesus Came into the World to Give an Example for Living._**
The apostle Peter said, "For you have been called for this purpose, since Christ also suffered for you, leaving you an example for you to follow in His steps" (1 Peter 2:21).

C. **_Jesus Came into the World to Destroy the Works of the Devil._**
The apostle John said, "The Son of God appeared for this purpose, to destroy the works of the devil" (1 John 3:8).

D. **_Jesus Came into the World to Provide a Sacrifice for Sin._** Paul said, "When the fullness of the time came, God sent forth His son, born of a woman, born under the law, so that He might redeem those who were under the law, that we might receive the adoption as sons" (Galatians 4:4-5).

Jesus emptied His deity into humanity and became obedient unto death, even death on the cross (see Philippians 2:1-11).

▶ FOR DISCUSSION

1. What is the origin of Jesus?

2. What does John 1:14 suggest about God?

3. What were some of the claims that Jesus made of Himself?

4. Why did Jesus come into the world?

Chapter 5

WHAT WE BELIEVE ABOUT THE HOLY SPIRIT
(John 14:25-26; 15:26)

When attempting to understand the Trinity–God the Father, God the Son, and God the Holy Spirit—the most misunderstood of the three is God the Holy Spirit. This is so because God the Father and God the Son are usually looked upon as persons. However, with God the Holy Spirit, He is most often referred to as a thing and not a person. This is definitely a misunderstanding of the Holy Spirit.

Also, the Holy Spirit is seen by most people as simply a power that moves upon the emotions of people at the time of a hot song, sermon, prayer, or testimony. But the Holy Spirit is a person who moves upon the person's intellect, emotions, and will.

In the above-referenced passages of Scripture, Jesus was in conference with His disciples. He was trying to prepare them for His coming death. Jesus wanted His disciples to know that His death was an absolute necessity.

The words of Jesus created sorrow in the hearts of His disciples. But Jesus gave them help and hope by assuring them that they would not have to go at life alone. He promised them that He would send them a Comforter, a Counselor, a Helper, a Companion, and an Advocate. The Greek word that is translated "comforter, counselor, or helper" is the word *paraketos*. This word means "one called alongside."

The Holy Spirit goes alongside the church and the individual believer to give help in the time of deepest need. He would also give help as the church continued the work that was begun by Jesus Christ during His earthly ministry.

I. The Holy Spirit in Creation (Genesis 1:2)

"The earth was formless and void, and darkness was over the surface of the deep; and the Spirit of God was moving over the surface of the waters."

It was the Holy Spirit's part in creation to give life and order to that which had been created. The Spirit of God moved upon the formless and empty earth and gave it its present order and beauty.

The Holy Spirit designed and empowered all creation to work together for the good of each part. The Spirit did not add any new elements to the world. He merely gave order to what was already there. Though the world had been created, that which had been created was unproductive until the Holy Spirit moved upon it.

It was the Holy Spirit's task to prepare humankind a pleasant place in which to live. So then, before humanity was created, the Holy Spirit gave order to all that God had created for him to enjoy.

II. The Holy Spirit's Indwelling of Old Testament Personalities

A careful examination of the Old Testament shows that the Holy Spirit indwelled certain people whom God chose to use in a very special way. It should also be understood that this indwelling was not necessarily permanent.

Joseph was elevated from slave to ruler in Egypt because of the indwelling Holy Spirit (see Genesis 41:38). Joshua was commissioned to be the successor of Moses because he was indwelled by the Holy Spirit (see Numbers 27:18). Daniel was able to interpret the dreams of King Nebuchadnezzar because of being indwelled by the Holy Spirit (see Daniel 4:8).

Samson became the mighty man he was because the Spirit of the Lord came upon him in a mighty way (see Judges 14:19). Samson experienced failure in life only when the Lord departed from him (see Judges 16:20). The Holy Spirit temporarily came upon Saul when he was anointed king of Israel (see 1 Samuel 11:5-11), and then left him when David was anointed by Samuel as king over Israel (see 1 Samuel 16:13-14).

III. The Holy Spirit in the Life of Jesus

When the angel Gabriel came to Mary to announce the birth of Jesus, he said to Mary, "The Holy Spirit will come upon you, and the power of the Most High will overshadow you; and for that reason the holy Child shall be called the Son of God" (Luke 1:35).

An angel of the Lord also appeared to Joseph and said, "Joseph, son of David, do not be afraid to take Mary as your wife; for the Child who has been conceived in her is of the Holy Spirit" (Matthew 1:20b).

Jesus was anointed by the Holy Spirit at the time of His baptism. "After being baptized, Jesus came up immediately from the water; and behold, the heavens were opened, and he saw the Spirit of God descending as a dove and lighting on Him, and behold, a voice out of the heavens said,'This is My beloved Son, in whom I am well-pleased'" (Matthew 3:16-17).

After His baptism, Jesus was "led up by the Spirit into the wilderness to be tempted by the devil" (Matthew 4:1).

After His temptation in the wilderness, "Jesus returned to Galilee in the power of the Spirit, and news about Him spread through all the surrounding district" (Luke 4:14).

Jesus went to Nazareth and went into the synagogue and publicly read the prophecy concerning His call to preach. Jesus said, "THE SPIRIT OF THE LORD IS UPON ME, BECAUSE HE ANOINTED ME TO PREACH THE GOSPEL TO THE POOR. HE HAS SENT ME TO PROCLAIM RELEASE TO THE CAPTIVES, AND RECOVERY OF SIGHT TO THE BLIND, TO SET FREE THOSE WHO ARE OPPRESSED, TO PROCLAIM THE FAVORABLE YEAR OF THE LORD" (Luke 4:18-19).

Jesus performed all His miracles by the power of the Holy Spirit. Jesus said to the Pharisees, "If I cast out demons by the Spirit of God, then the kingdom of God has come upon you" (Matthew 12:28).

Jesus practiced good works in the power of the Holy Spirit. The apostle Peter said about Jesus in his sermon to Cornelius, "God anointed him with the Holy Spirit and with power, and . . . he went about doing good" (Acts 10:38).

Jesus offered Himself as a sacrifice for sin in the power of the Spirit. The Hebrews writer said, "For if the blood of goats and bulls and the ashes of a heifer sprinkling those who have been defiled sanctify for the cleansing of the flesh, how much more will the blood of Christ, who through the eternal Spirit offered Himself without blemish to God, cleanse your conscience from dead works to serve the living God?" (Hebrews 9:13-14).

Jesus was raised from the grave by the power of the Holy Spirit. The apostle Paul said, "If the Spirit of Him who raised Jesus from the dead dwells in you, He who raised Christ Jesus from the dead will also give life to your mortal bodies through His Spirit who dwells in you" (Romans 8:11).

IV. The Holy Spirit in Regeneration

Many people are familiar with the part that grace and faith play in our regeneration, but some do not fully understand the Holy Spirit's work in the process of regeneration. Paul said, "For by grace you have been saved through faith" (Ephesians 2:8). Paul was suggesting that Jesus saves us by His unmerited favor, and this unmerited favor is received through faith in Jesus.

However, there is something else going on that is most often overlooked in the salvation process. The Holy Spirit is also at work. Jesus said to Nicodemus, "The wind blows where it wishes and you hear the sound of it, but do not know where it comes from and where it is going; so is everyone who is born of the Spirit" (John 3:8). These words suggest that regeneration is both a miracle and a mystery.

Destruction of the deeds of the flesh is assured by the help of the Holy Spirit. Paul advised the Galatians to walk in the Spirit in order for them not to carry out the desires of the flesh (see Galatians 5:16).

No one can walk in two directions at the same time. While a person is walking in the flesh, that person cannot be walking in the Spirit; and while we are walking in the Spirit we cannot walk in the flesh. The level of success that people experience in the Christian life is dependent upon the level of control they give the Holy Spirit in their lives.

The Holy Spirit dwells within the believer in order to produce fruit in the Christian life. "The fruit of the Spirit is love, joy, peace, patience, kindness, goodness, faithfulness, gentleness, self-control" (Galatians 5:22-23). This fruit is produced when the believer allows the Holy Spirit to control her or his life.

The Holy Spirit sanctifies the believer for the service of God. Sanctification begins at the very moment regeneration takes place. The Holy Spirit makes the believer a holy vessel, prepared to be used by the Lord (see 2 Thessalonians 2:13).

V. The Holy Spirit in the Church

It is important for us to understand that the Holy Spirit is active in the life of the church at times other than the worship hour. The Holy Spirit is also present and active in the church even when the activities may not seem to be highly emotional.

The Holy Spirit causes the church to become a spiritual fellowship. The Holy Spirit brings people together from all walks of life and makes them into one body, with Jesus Christ as the Head of the body.

The Holy Spirit keeps the church functioning as a church. It is only through the work of the Holy Spirit that the organization of the church becomes a living organism, moving at the Lord's command, and doing the Lord's will.

The Holy Spirit distributes spiritual gifts in the church for the common good of all (see 1 Corinthians 12:7). These gifts are given by grace and according to the sovereign will of God.

Through the work of the Holy Spirit God gives the church variety, and He gives the variety unity.

The Holy Spirit empowers the church to win the world for Jesus. Jesus said, "You will receive power when the Holy Spirit has come upon you; and you shall be My witnesses both in Jerusalem, and in all Judea and Samaria, and even to the remotest part of the earth" (Acts 1:8).

FOR DISCUSSION

1. What part did the Holy Spirit have in creation?
2. What is the work of the Holy Spirit in regeneration?
3. What is the work of the Holy Spirit in the life of the church?

Chapter 6

WHAT WE BELIEVE ABOUT THE BIBLE—Part 1
(Psalm 119:11; 2 Timothy 3:16-17)

There was a time when Satan attacked the church through gross immorality. But he seems to be doing more harm to the church through religion than he has ever done through immorality.

Satan is doing the church the very same way the enemies of Daniel did him. When the enemies of Daniel could not find fault in him at the point of his character, they attacked him at the point of his religion.

It is really strange that the black church could bring black people through slavery, segregation, and dehumanizing treatment, but now she is inadequate to meet the needs of people. Black people fail to realize that Satan is attacking the church at the point of religion.

The reason he is as successful as he is is because people are only casually familiar with the Bible.

The apostle Paul said, "All Scripture is inspired by God and profitable for teaching, for reproof, for correction, for training in righteousness; so that the man of God may be adequate, equipped for every good work" (2 Timothy 3:16-17).

It should be understood that the Scriptures to which Paul referred did not consist of the New Testament because the New Testament was still being written. Paul made reference to what is now known as the Old Testament only.

I. The Origin of the Bible

The Bible did not begin with the thoughts and ideas of men or angels. The Bible has its origin in God. Paul said, "All Scripture is inspired by God." This means that the Bible is God-breathed. Being God-breathed suggests that the Bible is filled up with God.

There is divine-human cooperation in the Bible; God is the Author and man is the writer. But it all began with God. The Bible comes directly from the mind of God. God intends for the Bible to direct people just as the chart and the compass direct ships on the sea.

II. The Value of the Bible

Paul said, "All Scripture is . . . profitable for teaching, for reproof, for correction, for training in righteousness; so that the man of God may be adequate, equipped for every good work" (2 Timothy 3:16-17).

It is evident that few people see the Bible as being valuable. This is so because so few people read and study the Bible. But the Bible provides teaching for guidance of a person's life. The Bible provides principles for everything that confronts man.

The Bible is also valuable for reproof. This means that the Bible is God's means of convicting humanity of sin. But to be convicted of sin is not enough. Therefore, the Bible is also valuable for correction. After discovering one's wrong, the next thing is to find some means of getting right. After a person gets right through the Bible, the Bible also helps that person to stay right by training in righteousness.

III. The Power of the Bible

David said, "Your word I have treasured in my heart, That I may not sin against You" (Psalm 119:11).

David treasured the Word of God in his heart; thus, it was hidden from public view. It is not easy to forget that which has been treasured. As long as the Word of God was treasured in the heart of David, that meant the Word occupied his affections and his understanding.

David understood the power of the Word of God, so he treasured it in his heart and not just his head. The heart is the seat of the emotions. Solomon said, "Out of [the heart] are the issues of life" (Proverbs 4:23, KJV).

The heart is also the seat of the will and moral life. Until the will is changed, the person will never be changed. David knew the power of the Word of God, so he treasured it in his heart. When the life is brought in line with the Word of God, the will is made to conform to the will of God.

David also saw treasuring the Word of God as a means of not sinning against God. David knew that as long as he was guided by the Word of God he could not be guided by the will of the devil or his flesh.

David was aware that either God's Word would keep a person from sinning, or sinning would keep a person from God's Word. As long as Eve kept the Word of God by faith, she resisted the devil. But the very moment she began to doubt the Word of God, she was caught by the devil.

▶ FOR DISCUSSION

1. How did the Bible become the Bible?

2. What value does the Bible have?

3. What impact can the Bible have on one's relationship with God?

Chapter 7

WHAT WE BELIEVE ABOUT THE BIBLE—Part 2
(2 Timothy 3:16-17)

The Bible has been attacked and ridiculed by the enemies of Christianity. It has been challenged by science, philosophy, and history. Yet, the Bible still stands as the greatest book that has ever been written.

There is much ignorance of the Bible. This ignorance is evidenced by neglect of the Bible. There are not very many people who do not have at least one Bible in their houses, yet very few of these people read and study the Bible with any regularity.

People for the most part give the Bible a marginal place in their lives, wherein it deserves to be central. The Bible deserves a new chance to bless their lives.

Since the beginning of time, there have been numerous books written by many different people. But no book that has ever been written can compare with the Bible. The Bible is a book unlike any other book. The word *Bible* comes from the Greek word *biblos*, which means "book or scroll."

The Bible has many writers, yet it has only one author, and that is God the Holy Spirit. The Bible was written over a period of about fifteen hundred years. It was first written in Hebrew and Greek, with small portions of the Old Testament written in Aramaic.

I. An Inspired Book

"All Scripture is inspired by God...."

To say that the Bible is an inspired book is to say that the Bible is God-breathed. The Bible is produced by God. It has the breath of God in it. The apostle Peter said, "For no prophecy was ever made by an act of human will, but men moved by the Holy Spirit spoke from God" (2 Peter 1:21).

Inspiration is the result of the power of God working on, in, or through those who are inspired. Inspiration produces in the inspired that which would not be possible with human knowledge and emotions alone.

There is no way that human knowledge and emotions could have the writers of the Bible writing about events that occurred hundreds of years before they came on the scene or hundreds of years into the future.

Only the inspiration of God could have Moses writing about the creation of the world many years after it occurred, and Isaiah writing about the suffering and death of Jesus seven hundred years before He suffered and died.

There is assurance that the Bible is an inspired book because human beings would have never written a book that would paint such a dreadful picture of humankind and such a strange source of salvation for fallen humanity.

II. A Revealed Book

The word *reveal* means "an unveiling, or drawing back the veil." Where the Bible is concerned, God is making known what would have been concealed. In the book of Revelation, God gives glimpses of Himself, His will, and His truth.

In the book of Revelation, God communicates the truth about Himself for a special purpose or end. All revelation comes from God and is concerned with God. In the Bible, God unveils Himself to man. The Bible tells what only God knows. It is not a record of people's opinions, ideas, or thoughts.

If there is to be revelation, there must be fellowship with God. God does not reveal Himself to the unsaved in the same way and at the same level that He does to those who walk with Him day after day.

The revelation of the Bible is progressive in nature. Those who wrote the New Testament had a clearer revelation of God than those who wrote the Old. The Old Testament is the background and the New Testament explains the Old.

Nature and history revealed some things about God, but the Bible reveals the full nature and purpose of God. It is because of this revelation of the nature and purpose of God that humanity can worship God in Spirit and in truth.

III. An Influential Book

The influence of the Bible does not stay within the hearts of those who believe. The Bible has never been anywhere that it has not effected change in the lives of people and nations.

Because of the influence of the Bible, sinners have been changed to saints; the sorrowful have been given joy; and courage has been given to those who have been discouraged. The Bible helps people to live with one another in a positive way. The Spirit of the Bible undermines broken relationships and transforms life as yeast causes dough to become light and fluffy.

The laws of the land have been influenced by the Bible. Take away the Bible and there would be nothing to give guidance to the laws given by government and lived out by society. The Bible is a chart to show the way of life. Those who live according to the teachings of the Bible will have fewer problems living according to the laws of the land.

It should be understood that the Bible is not to be worshipped. But it is to be a guide to bring people to the God of the Bible.

IV. A Sufficient Book

The Bible is a sufficient principle of faith and practice. It makes the way of salvation so plain that even a fool has no reason to be lost.

The Bible provides God's plan for His church. There will never be a time when a person or the church as a whole will outgrow the Bible. The Bible is an ageless book. It provides a message from the unchanging Lord that speaks to the needs of people in an ever-changing world.

The Bible was written to meet the needs of humans. It was not written for angels or by angels. It is a book that was written for humanity. The major concern of the Bible is the relationship that goes on between God and man.

The Bible stands as the permanent and final record of how God made known His redeeming love and grace to humanity through Christ Jesus.

As long as humanity has the Bible, there is no need for the *New World Translation of the Scriptures* that is used by the Jehovah's Witnesses. As long as humanity has the Bible, there is no need for the Holy Koran that is used by the Muslims.

As long as humanity has the Bible, there is no need for the *Doctrine and Covenants*, *The Pearl of Great Price*, and *The Book of Mormons*—all used by the Mormons.

Centuries have come and gone, but the Bible still stands. Kings are crowned and kings are dethroned; presidents are elected and presidents are defeated—but the Bible still stands. Unbelief abandons the Bible, atheism speaks against it, yet the Bible still stands.

The prophet Isaiah said, "The grass withers, the flower fades, But the Word of our God stands forever" (Isaiah 40:8).

▶ FOR DISCUSSION

1. What is the most common attitude toward the Bible, and what is the result of that attitude?

2. How can the Bible be described?

3. What did Paul suggest is the purpose of the Scriptures?

Chapter 8

WHAT WE BELIEVE ABOUT THE FALL OF MAN
(Genesis 3)

After God created Adam and Eve, He placed them in the Garden of Eden to become keepers of it and to cultivate it (see Genesis 2:15). They were given freedom to eat fruit from all the trees in the Garden except the Tree of the Knowledge of Good and Evil. God told them that the day they ate of that tree they would die.

Adam disobeyed God and ate fruit from the tree from which he was forbidden to eat. Adam's disobedience caused him to fall from his state of innocence into a state of sin. However, God did not give up on or abandon Adam. He remained faithful to Adam by providing for him salvation from sin.

I. The Fall of Man
  A. *Giving Attention to the Wrong Advice*
  Man's fall from his state of innocence began when Eve gave her attention to the teachings of the devil. Eve was convinced by the devil that God did not mean all that He said. The devil made Eve believe that God was jealous of Adam and her.

  The devil told Eve, "You surely shall not die! For God knows that in the day you eat from it your eyes will be opened, and you will be like God, knowing good and evil" (Genesis 3:4-5).

  Eve began to doubt God's love and concern. She thought God was trying to hold her back from becoming all that she could be. Therefore, "When the woman saw that the tree was good for food, and that it was a delight to the eyes, and that the tree was desirable to make one wise, she took from its fruit and ate; and she gave also to her husband with her, and he ate" (Genesis 3:6).

After listening to what the devil had to say, Eve began reasoning within herself and judging the situation by the outward appearance. She saw that the tree from which God had forbidden her to eat was one of tasty fruit, beautiful appearance, and a provider of knowledge.

There was somewhat of a progression involved in the fall of man. Eve saw, she took, she ate, and she gave. As she looked at the forbidden tree, her desire for its fruit began to set in. Once desire had set in, Eve took some of the fruit from the tree in order to satisfy her desires.

Then Eve was not satisfied with being disobedient to God all by herself, so she gave some of the fruit to Adam her husband, and he ate.

Once Adam had eaten of the forbidden fruit, the eyes of both Adam and Eve were opened, and they knew that they were naked.

B. *The Helplessness of Self-righteousness*
Once Adam and Eve had developed for themselves a very serious problem, they did what the average person would do: they sought to solve the problem without any outside help. Adam and Eve sewed fig leaves together in order to cover their nakedness. This was an attempt to cover sin rather than to confess it.

The apostle John said, "If we confess our sins, He is faithful and righteous to forgive us our sins and to cleanse us from all unrighteousness" (1 John 1:9).

Self-righteousness is helpless in dealing with sin because it turns the self farther toward the self. Sin begins with selfishness, and self-righteousness suggests that self is the answer to its own problems. This attitude adds to the problem of sin rather than alleviating it.

When Adam and Eve discovered that sin and self-righteousness were displeasing to God, they attempted to hide themselves from God by hiding among the trees. Rather than walking in the presence of God, sin had them attempting to hide from the presence of God.

The actions of Adam and Eve show the power of the guilt of sin. It will have you running from the presence of God rather than running to God.

Adam also showed his self-righteousness by not taking full blame for his actions. He blamed both God and Eve for his act of sin. Adam said to God, "The woman whom You gave to be with me, she gave me from the tree, and I ate" (Genesis 3:12).

Adam blamed God for his actions by suggesting that if God had not given him the woman then the woman would not have been able to give him the fruit.

II. God Seeking Adam

After Adam and Eve had come to the realization that they had fallen from their state of innocence and brought displeasure to the heart of God, they sought to flee from the presence of God. But God showed His faithfulness to humanity by looking for Adam in the cool of the day (see Genesis 3:8).

The attitude and actions of God exemplified His grace. God called out to Adam and said, "Where are you?" (Genesis 3:9). Since God knows everything, it is important to understand that God did not raise this question for His own sake, but rather for the sake of Adam. Adam needed to know that he was in a state of sin, self-righteousness, and separation from God.

In spite of the separating power of sin, God knows that a person's life is empty and void without Him. This is why God looked for Adam. God knew that if He had not gone looking for Adam, Adam would have never gone looking for Him.

God showed His love for humanity by providing it with a source of salvation from its sins. God promised Adam that because of his sin he would experience suffering and sorrow.

But God also promised a Savior that would come from the seed of the woman. This Savior would bruise the head of the serpent, and the serpent would bruise the heel of the Savior. The gospel of Luke traces Jesus Christ all the way back to Seth, the son of Adam and Eve (see Genesis 4:25; Luke 3:38).

As a foreshadowing of what God would do to save those who trust Him, God made garments of skin to clothe Adam and Eve (see Genesis 3:21). This was a picture of the atonement. The word *atonement* means "to cover."

In order for Adam and Eve's nakedness to be covered, the animal had to give its life. In order for humanity's sin to be covered, Jesus gave His life.

▶ FOR DISCUSSION

1. Why were Adam and Eve placed in the Garden of Eden?

2. What was an important factor in the beginning of man's fall?

3. How did man first deal with his fall?

4. How did God deal with man's fall?

Chapter 9

WHAT WE BELIEVE ABOUT SALVATION
(Acts 16:30-31)

Being saved carries with it the idea of restoration from sickness or danger. The unsaved have no healing for a soul that is sick and no help for a soul that is in danger of being lost in hell.

The importance of what is believed about salvation can never be underestimated. What is believed about salvation determines the approach to receiving it and sharing it.

For instance, if people believe (as some religious people do) that in order to be saved they must hang over hell on a spider web, or hear angels or voices above their heads, then they will never be saved according to what the Bible teaches about salvation.

Or, if they believe that in order to be saved they must be baptized, then they could never be saved on their deathbeds, for instance, if they could not be baptized.

If persons believe they can be saved through their works then they will always find themselves working in order to gain favor with God; and if they fail in their efforts to please Him through their works then they believe they have no salvation.

The apostle Paul said, "If you confess with your mouth Jesus as Lord, and believe in your heart that God raised Him from the dead, you will be saved" (Romans 10:9).

There are many approaches and beliefs concerning what it takes to be saved. But it is important to consider what the Bible teaches concerning the gift of salvation. Salvation is a gift because humanity has no adequate exchange for it. Paul said, "For the wages of sin is death, but the free gift of God is eternal life in Christ Jesus our Lord" (Romans 6:23).

I. Man Is Helpless in Saving Himself (Acts 16:31)

Paul said to the jailer, "Believe in the Lord Jesus, and you will be saved" (Acts 16:31).

The King James Version reads, "Believe on the Lord Jesus"; and the New American Standard Bible reads, "Believe in the Lord Jesus." Though the two seem to differ, they are actually similar.

Car drivers are familiar with the fact that cars have brakes. The brakes are made to slow down and stop the car. The reason why people willingly drive their cars is because they believe the brakes will slow down and stop the car when needed. For that reason the driver believes in the brakes.

But when drivers come to a red light, or stop sign, or some danger in the path and they put their feet on the brake pedal and apply pressure, they believe on the brakes because they trust the brakes to do what they were designed to do.

There is no salvation in thinking about the Lord Jesus, talking about Him, or dreaming about Him; salvation comes by believing on Him or in Him.

II. Works Are Powerless in Saving the Unsaved (Ephesians 2:8, 9)

"For by grace you have been saved through faith . . . not as a result of works, so that no one should boast."

The tense of the verb phrase "have been saved" is the perfect tense in the Greek. This suggests a completed action with a continuous effect. Paul was literally saying to the Ephesians, "For by grace you have been saved and you stand saved."

The reason why works are powerless in saving the sinner is because the sinner has both good and bad works, and if he or she would put both the good and the bad on the scales, the bad would outweigh the good.

Either people are busy doing what they should not be doing, or they are so busy that they are not doing what they should be doing; or they are sitting idly by and letting opportunities to do good slip away.

Christians are not Christians because they have performed so many good works, but Christians are Christians by grace plus nothing. And they are saved for the purpose of performing good works.

III. Without Salvation, the Unsaved Are Eternally Lost (Luke 16:19-31)

In the present time, each person is building for self a character that will carry him or her into the future. What a person is today he or she will be more of tomorrow. As the lost continue to live lost lives, they become more lost, because the older a person gets the more difficult it becomes for him or her to accept Christ as Savior and Lord.

Hell is eternal and unalterable. Once a person dies there is no second chance at this life. The rich man who died and went to hell in Luke 16 discovered that there was an impassable gulf that separated him from the paradise of God in heaven.

The only way this gulf could be passed was to live in this world and at some point trust Christ as Savior and Lord before death. Otherwise, there would be an immediate arrival in hell—for when the rich man died, he lifted up his eyes in hell and was in torment.

There are those persons who feel that God is too gracious to send anybody to hell. In fact, it is true that it is not the Lord's desire that anyone should go to hell. The apostle Peter said concerning the Lord's desire for humanity's salvation, "The Lord is not slow about His promise, as some count slowness, but is patient toward you, not wishing for any to perish but for all to come to repentance" (2 Peter 3:9).

Jesus said to Nicodemus, "He who believes in Him is not judged; he who does not believe has been judged already, because he has not believed in the name of the only begotten Son of God" (John 3:18).

IV. In Salvation the Saved Are Justified (Romans 5:1-2)

Paul said, "Therefore, having been justified by faith, we have peace with God through our Lord Jesus Christ, through whom also we have obtained our introduction by faith into this grace in which we stand; and we exult in hope of the glory of God."

Justification is a legal term that expresses at least two things. First of all, justification says that the individual is guilty of a wrong. Second, justification says that though the person is guilty of wrong, that person is set free because Jesus gave His life on Calvary's cross.

Justification suggests that the believer has been reconciled to God. Paul said, "God was in Christ reconciling the world to Himself, not counting their trespasses against them" (2 Corinthians 5:19b).

In justification the saved receive the righteousness of Jesus Christ. Paul said, "He made Him who knew no sin to be sin on our behalf, so that we might become the righteousness of God in Him" (2 Corinthians 5:21).

To be saved is to be delivered from the penalty of all sins. To be saved is to be delivered from the power of those sins which do so easily entangle man. To be saved is to be delivered from the grasp of the devil and hell. To be saved is to be adopted from being a child of the devil and to become a child of God. To be saved is to be free from condemnation and stand justified before God.

Paul told the church at Rome, "Therefore there is now no condemnation for those who are in Christ Jesus" (Romans 8:1).

▶ FOR DISCUSSION

1. What does it mean to be saved?

2. What part do works have in the process of salvation?

3. What is the result of not being saved?

4. What does it mean to be justified?

Chapter
10

WHAT WE BELIEVE ABOUT
THE ETERNAL SECURITY OF THE BELIEVER
(John 10:27-29; 2 Timothy 1:12)

Out of all the many things believed and practiced as Baptists, the doctrine that probably creates the most uncertainty in the minds of Christians is the eternal security of the believer. This is so because not all Christians believe that all Christians are saved eternally. Christians are not sure of the eternal security of the believer because of their sins and ignorance of or a lack of faith in the Lord's work in salvation.

The issue of "once saved, always saved" is one that probably causes more doubt in the hearts and minds of believers than anything else taught and practiced in the Baptist church. Many people have been Baptist Christians for many years, yet they have difficulty handling the issue of eternal security. They have difficulty believing it and because they have difficulty believing it, they have even greater difficulty teaching it and preaching it.

The cause of the difficulties in believing in the principle of "once saved, always saved" can be attributed to a misunderstanding of several biblical passages. One in particular is Galatians 5:4. In this passage, Paul said, "You have been severed from Christ, you who are seeking to be justified by law; you have fallen from grace."

If this verse were taken by itself without any consideration of the context in which it was written, it would seem to strongly support the idea of one's losing his or her salvation. In reality, this verse is actually teaching the superiority of salvation by grace over supposed salvation by the Law.

When the Galatians were saved, they were saved by grace. But the time came when they felt that salvation by grace was not secure like salvation by the works of the Law. Therefore, they attempted to keep the Law of Moses as an added security to salvation by grace. But anything mixed with grace dilutes the grace and renders it ineffective.

When Paul received word of the actions of the Galatians, he suggested to them that when they tried to make salvation a reward of keeping the Law, they had fallen from the realm of grace and back into the realm of the Law.

He was not suggesting that they had lost their salvation. He was merely stating that they were seeking salvation from a source lower than that from which it came.

When engaged in discussions about the eternal security of the believer, or "once saved, always saved," there are numerous scriptural passages that support this fact. This lesson shall examine a few of these passages to see what they say and mean. As these passages are studied, it should be done with an open mind and a desire to hear what the Lord has to say.

I. Salvation as a New Birth (John 3:6-7)

As Jesus talked to Nicodemus one night, He said to him, "That which is born of the flesh is flesh, and that which is born of the Spirit is spirit. Do not be amazed that I said to you, 'You must be born again'" (John 3:6-7).

Jesus wanted Nicodemus to know that salvation means that a person receives a new birth. This new birth is not from earth but rather from above. It is a birth that is the product of the work of the Holy Spirit. In spite of people's not acting spiritual at times, it does not alter the fact that all who are Christians are born of the Spirit.

The apostle Paul also referred to the new birth as transformation. Paul said to the Romans, "Do not be conformed to this world, but be transformed by the renewing of your mind" (Romans 12:2b).

The Greek word that is translated "transformed" is the word from which comes the English word *metamorphosis*. The metamorphosis to which Paul referred is a change that occurs by supernatural means. It suggests a change in appearance, condition, character, and function.

Metamorphosis is what a caterpillar goes through when it changes into a butterfly. Once that caterpillar has become a butterfly, it will never know again what it will be like to be a caterpillar, because it will die a butterfly. The reason for this is that its nature has been changed. It has been transformed.

Salvation is a new birth and is eternally secure because once a person is born, he or she cannot get unborn.

II. Salvation as an Eternal Gift (John 3:16)

As Jesus continued His conversation with Nicodemus, He assured Nicodemus that salvation was not of human origin. Salvation is a gift from God through Jesus Christ. Jesus said to Nicodemus, "For God so loved the world, that He gave His only begotten Son, that whoever believes in Him shall not perish, but have eternal life" (John 3:16).

When Jesus gave His life on Calvary He did not do so to give temporary life. He died to give eternal life. Eternal life is life that has no beginning and no ending. It does have a beginning in the one saved, but it does not have a beginning in its being. Once a person is saved, eternal life sets in forever. There is nothing that that person or anyone else can do to stop the process of eternal life once it has begun.

The reason eternal life is a gift is because man has no adequate exchange for its purchase. Man does not have the possessions, the power, or the position to gain eternal life. It is a gift from God through Jesus Christ. If salvation is the gift of eternal life, then the salvation of the believer is eternally secure.

III. Salvation Preserved by One's Relationship to Jesus (John 15:1-6)

In John 15, Jesus is seen in conference with His disciples as He nears the close of His earthly ministry. As Jesus talked with His disciples, He made the claim of being the True Vine.

In verse 2 of this chapter, Jesus made a statement that people often use as proof that salvation can be lost. In verse 2, Jesus said, "Every branch in Me that does not bear fruit, He takes away; and every branch that bears fruit, He prunes it so that it may bear more fruit."

It should be understood that this verse does not deal with the loss of salvation but rather with the loss of power or effectiveness. Jesus further stated, "If anyone does not abide in Me, he is thrown away as a branch and dries up; and they gather them, and cast them into the fire and they are burned" (John 15:6).

A broken fellowship with Jesus does not mean that the relationship has been severed. Every branch that receives its life from Jesus, the true Vine, will maintain life through Him, but not every branch will bring forth fruit. Every branch that will bring forth fruit is given special care by the Vinedresser because He prunes it that it may bring forth more fruit.

IV. Salvation as Protection for God's Sheep (John 10:27-29)

One of the finest passages of Scripture on the eternal security of the believer is the passage from John 10:27-29. In this passage, Jesus says that He has personal knowledge of each of His sheep. Jesus said, "I know them" (see verse 27). Jesus was suggesting by these words that He knew His sheep by name and He knew their nature.

To know someone is more than knowing that person's name. It also means knowing his or her conduct and his or her character.

Not only does Jesus know His sheep personally, but He also said that He personally gives each one eternal life. Jesus said, "I give eternal life to them." The receivers of this eternal life did not buy it; they did not earn it; they did not find it; nor did they produce it from within themselves. It is a gift from Jesus Christ.

Not only does Jesus know His sheep personally, and not only does He give them eternal life, but also Jesus said concerning His sheep, "They shall never perish." The Christian shall never perish because the Christian life is a life of eternality.

Jesus also dealt with the security of the believer in the words, "No one will snatch them out of My hand. My Father, who has given them to Me, is greater than all; and no one is able to snatch them out of the Father's hand" (John 10:28b-29).

Salvation is eternally secure because of who holds the Christian. The Christian is in the hand of Jesus and the hand of Jesus is in the hand of God. God is greater than everything the child of God encounters in life; and since the Christian is in the hand of God, that guarantees his or her safety and security forever—for no one is able to snatch the Christian out of the hand of Jesus or God. Some may try, but none are successful in the effort.

Since the Christian is in the hand of both God and Jesus, the Christian cannot be snatched out; a believer cannot fall out; nor can the child of God walk out. He or she is safe forever.

V. The Saved as Predestined to Salvation (Ephesians 1:4-5)

The salvation of the saved was predetermined before the world was ever created. This was accomplished because of the foreknowledge of God. God intimately knew all those He would save before they ever came on the scene; and since He calls His own unto Himself, He gave us power to become His children. Paul said to the Ephesians, "Just as he chose us in Him before the foundation of the world, that we would be holy and blameless before Him. In love He predestined us to adoption as sons through Jesus Christ to Himself, according to the kind intention of His will" (Ephesians 1:4-5).

For God to predetermine salvation and then not be able to keep us saved would mean that God's promises cannot be trusted. If God could fail His beloved at the point of securing salvation, He could also fail us at the point of supplying all our needs.

Paul said to the Romans, "For whom He foreknew, He also predestined to become conformed to the image of His Son, so that He would be the firstborn among many brethren; and these whom He predestined, He also called; and these whom He called, He also justified; and these whom He justified, He also glorified" (Romans 8:29-30).

God's activity in the process of salvation is worth notice. He foreknew, He predestined, He called, He justified, and He glorified. It is worth noting that all of these things are in the past tense.

God knew each person before he or she arrived on the scene. God predestined before He created. God invited humanity to salvation and He justified them after their response to His calling. Finally, He glorified us after we were justified. The saved person's glorification is already secured in Jesus Christ.

VI. Salvation Secured by the Holy Spirit (Ephesians 1:13-14; 4:30)
Salvation is secured by the work of the Holy Spirit. The apostle Paul was inspired to write, "In Him, you also, after listening to the message of truth, the gospel of your salvation—having also believed, you were sealed in Him with the Holy Spirit of promise, who is given as a pledge of our inheritance, with a view to the redemption of God's own possession, to the praise of His glory" (Ephesians 1:13-14).

Here Paul spoke of the Holy Spirit in two ways in relationship to salvation. First of all, Paul described the Holy Spirit as a seal. A seal shows ownership, and it also suggests safety.

In the process of salvation, the Holy Spirit is given to stamp the believer as the property of God. He is also given to keep the Christian safe as medicine is kept safe in order to be consumed by the sick. The sealing of the Holy Spirit makes the Christian tamper-proof.

Second, the apostle Paul described the Holy Spirit as a "pledge of inheritance with a view to the redemption of God's own possession." This pledge carries the idea of earnest money being paid to hold something for the purchaser until the final payment can be made.

The Holy Spirit is holding man's salvation secure until Jesus Christ can return and carry him back to heaven.

VII. Salvation More Secure than a Double Lock (Colossians 3:3)
Everyone can appreciate the value of a lock. When people leave home, they lock themselves out and hope they have locked others out of their houses at the same time. When they return home they lock themselves in and hope they have locked others out at the same time. Most people have more than one lock on each door of

their house or apartment. People do this because they are trying to make themselves secure in this world. But in spite of their efforts, many people have still experienced break-ins.

But where salvation is concerned, there is a lock provided that can never be broken. Paul said to the Colossians, "For you have died and your life is hidden with Christ in God" (Colossians 3:3). To be hidden is to be out of sight. The Christian is out of sight with Christ when he or she is saved. That is the first lock. Just being hidden with Christ is security enough to keep anybody saved forever; but the Christian is hidden with Christ in God.

VIII. Salvation as a Deposit Made in a Bank (2 Timothy 1:12)

In this passage from the book of 2 Timothy, Paul used money's being deposited into a bank as a symbol of eternal security. No one in his or her right mind would put his or her money in a bank knowing that the bank was about to close.

Wherever people put their money, they want it to be there when they get ready for it. Therefore, when they put their money in a bank, they are saying that they believe in that bank. But when people are saved, they are doing something more important than putting money in a bank. They trust Jesus Christ to keep their souls saved while they live in a world of sin and sorrow.

Paul said, "I know whom I have believed and I am convinced that He is able to guard what I have entrusted to Him until that day" (2 Timothy 1:12b).

Christians are not kept because they have earned the right to be kept. They are not kept because they deserve it. Their being kept depends upon God's goodness and faithfulness to His promises. Jesus said, "All that the Father gives Me will come to Me, and the one who comes to Me I will certainly not cast out" (John 6:37).

FOR DISCUSSION

1. In what sense is salvation seen as a new birth?

2. What are some reasons why salvation of the soul is a permanent act?

3. What part do God the Father and God the Son have in the security of the believer?

Chapter 11

WHAT WE BELIEVE ABOUT THE CHURCH
(Matthew 16:18)

The words spoken here by Jesus were spoken at Caesarea Philippi. Caesarea Philippi possessed a cave where a shrine had been built in honor of idol gods. The population of Caesarea Philippi was largely pagan. With all of the paganism and idolatry in Caesarea Philippi, Jesus made an important announcement. The announcement was not a new announcement; it was just a new Announcer.

With there being all kinds of deities being worshipped in Caesarea Philippi, the people were accustomed to assemblies being called together. So, then, the word translated "church" in Matthew 16:18 was not a new word; Jesus just gave it a new significance.

At first glance, the words of this subject seem unimportant because there is the understanding among most people that there is only one church. This is true to a degree, but there needs to be an examination of the word that is translated "church" in Matthew 16:18.

The word translated "church" in Matthew 16:18 is the Greek word *ecclesia*. This word means "called out." Among the Greeks, an *ecclesia* was an assembly of free citizens called out from their homes and places of business to give consideration to matters of public interest.

Therefore, Jesus used a common word to make an uncommon announcement. "Upon this rock I will build my church; and the gates of hell shall not prevail against it."

The possessive pronoun "my" separates the called-out assembly of Jesus from all of the others.

Since the assembly Jesus called out was different from all of the others of His day and is to be different today, this lesson shall focus on the church. There are several things about the church to consider.

I. The Work of the Church

Christ gave His church a task which was different from that of any other called-out assembly. The church has the task of winning the lost for Christ. No, it is not the business of the church to save souls because she does not have any saving power.

Jesus said concerning the coming of the Holy Spirit, "Ye shall receive power, after that the Holy Ghost is come upon you: and ye shall be witnesses unto me both in Jerusalem, and in all Judea, and in Samaria, and unto the uttermost part of the earth" (Acts 1:8, KJV).

The church should be missionary in its praying, its teaching, its preaching, its giving, and its living. The whole life of the church should have a missionary flavor.

Robert H. Glover, in his book *The Bible Basis of Missions*, says the following concerning the early church in Jerusalem:

> The church had its gatherings for worship and fellowship, and its doctrinal preaching and teaching for the instruction and edification of its members . . . and all the so-called means of grace; not to mention its material edifices and equipment. But none of these, nor yet the sum of them all was meant to be regarded as the church's mission. . . . The church was not designed to be a reservoir, ever receiving and retaining for itself God's spiritual blessings, but rather a conduit conveying them on and out to others everywhere.

The work of the church is to fight against sin and Satan. But rather than the church fighting against sin and Satan, she finds herself being used by Satan and fighting against one another.

In the beginning of the church, each member was overwhelmed with the missionary spirit.

Each member understood what the work of the church really was. Many churches today need to go on a diet and trim the fat of trivial activities.

II. The Power of the Church

As Jesus prepared to ascend to the right hand of His Father after His resurrection, He said to His disciples, "Tarry ye in the city of Jerusalem, until ye be endued with power from on high" (Luke 24:49b, KJV).

They did what Jesus told them to do, and on the Day of Pentecost they received that power and their lives influenced others in a way like never before. The same kind of power is needed today.

As important as human resources might be, a church without spiritual power is not an effective church.

Large budgets, beautiful buildings, well-planned church calendars, well-trained choirs, church auxiliaries, and church leaders may aid in winning the world for Christ, but all of those things are useless without spiritual power.

One of the main reasons why the church of today is lacking in power is that she has ceased to pray. The church makes her greatest progress on her knees. Churches are still alive not because of their business meetings, but because of their prayer meetings.

The reason why the spiritual progress of the church of today is slower than the progress in the church of Jerusalem is because people today are too busy or too indifferent to pray. It is prayer that keeps the church in touch with the throne of God.

Through prayer, the church receives energy and power. Through this energy and power, she knows no defeat and continues to move forward in spite of the odds.

III. The Foundation of the Church

The church is built upon a firm foundation because Jesus built it upon Himself. When Jesus said, "Upon this rock I will build my church," He did not say He would build it upon Peter or any of his successors.

If Christ had built His church upon Peter or any of the other apostles or disciples, the foundation would have been frail and insecure.

The prophet Isaiah prophesied concerning the foundation on which the church would be built some seven hundred years before Christ came. "Behold, I lay in Zion for a foundation a stone, a tried stone, a precious corner stone, a sure foundation" (Isaiah 28:16, KJV).

The apostle Paul understood the stability of the church as he wrote to the Corinthians, "For other foundation can no man lay than that is laid, which is Jesus Christ" (1 Corinthians 3:11, KJV). All that the church is and stands for is built upon Christ. Christ is a sure foundation that will not give way.

Whenever there is talk about the foundation of the church, the words of Samuel J. Stone become more meaningful.

> The Church's one foundation,
> Is Jesus Christ her Lord;
> She is His new creation,
> By Spirit and the Word.
> From heaven He came and sought her,
> To be His holy bride;
> With His own blood He bought her,
> And for her life He died.

Look again at the words of Isaiah as he prophesied concerning the foundation of the church. "Behold, I lay in Zion for a foundation a stone, a tried stone, a precious corner stone, a sure foundation."

A. God Himself is the Contractor.
"Behold, I lay."

B. The material for the stone is made by God.
"Behold, I lay in Zion for a foundation a stone."

C. The foundation stone has been tested.
"Behold, I lay in Zion for a foundation a stone, a tried stone."

The writer of the book of Hebrews said about Jesus, "We have not an high priest which cannot be touched with the feeling of our infirmities; but was in all points tempted like as we are, yet without sin" (Hebrews 4:15, KJV).

D. **The foundation stone was the best that could be found.**
"Behold, I lay in Zion for a foundation stone . . . a precious corner stone." The Lord is a precious stone because He is the source of salvation.

E. **The stone is a sure foundation.**
"Behold, I lay in Zion for a foundation a stone . . . a sure foundation." This foundation stone was planned in eternity and was laid in the incarnation.

IV. The Church as the Body of Christ

The church is the body of Christ, with Christ as the Head. Paul said in 1 Corinthians 12:27 (KJV), "Now ye are the body of Christ, and members in particular." It is impossible for a cult to be the church and the church to be a cult. A body with two heads would be a monstrosity, and so would a head with two bodies. The world has had many churches, but Christ has only one.

As the church, the members are all united by one Spirit, and it includes all members who have their own functions.

As the church, all of the members are interdependent. Paul said, "The eye cannot say unto the hand, I have no need of thee: nor again the head to the feet, I have no need of you" (1 Corinthians 12:21, KJV). Each member of the body needs the help of the others. The church ought to praise God for the gifts of other members when the work of the Lord is being helped. It should not matter which member has the special gift, so long as the will of the Head is being done through the body.

As the body of Christ, the church is visible proof of the Lord's presence. The presence of a living body is the evidence of the presence of a living invisible Spirit. Every Christian is a witness to the living Christ, as surely as a living hand proves a living head.

As the body of Christ, each member is dependent upon the head. Without the head, which is Christ, the body is nothing more than a lifeless, corrupt corpse. The body exists for the head and not the head for the body. From the head each member receives its authority. If the hand is able to perform any skillful work, it is because the head has imparted wisdom and knowledge.

As the body of Christ, the church is an instrument of service. The body is the servant of the head; the church is the servant of Christ. The head has no way of working out its purposes except through the body. Just imagine what could be accomplished through the church if every member were fully yielded to the will of Christ, the Head.

As the body of Christ, the church cannot see corruption. The body of Jesus was a type of His church. His body was abused, bruised, and broken, but it did not see corruption.

The church as the body of Christ may be marred and outwardly weak, but as surely as the body of Jesus was transfigured, so shall His body, the church, be transformed on resurrection morning with the glory of God.

Just as the Head of the body, Jesus Christ, has ascended to heaven the body, which is the church, shall one day be caught up to meet Him.

When Christ was born into the world He was born at a time when sin was raging. He came to give the world hope in a time of hopelessness. Christ placed unlimited value on human life. One reason why Christ established His church was to fight against the evil forces in the world. He is still establishing and commissioning churches to enter into conflict with evil forces.

The challenge and opportunity today demand that churches be at their best. The church has to express herself in actions as well as words. A church can express herself best when she understands whose she is and who she is.

An important factor in the church's being at her best is her members' being able to recognize the church and distinguish it from cults and other groups that have organized in the name of religion.

It is important not to confuse the church with cults. There are several things which characterize a cult: (1) cult leaders claim authority by a direct revelation from God; (2) in the cult, salvation is by works rather than by grace through faith; (3) in the cult, there is often financial abuse; (4) in the cult, there is an uncertain system of doctrine; (5) those who do not believe in the uncertain system of doctrine are condemned as evil; (6) members are given special secret information; (7) cults prey on known Christians and church members; and (8) there is even an extrabiblical authority.

V. The Church as the Bride of Christ

The metaphor of the church as the bride of Christ implies submission to the authority of Christ. It implies both for the Lord and the church mutual possession and comradery. That is why any group which gathers in the name of the church and leaves Jesus out is not really the church.

In fact, any group that gathers in the name of the church and lifts the Holy Spirit above Christ is not the church Christ built. Jesus said concerning the Holy Spirit, "When the Comforter is come . . . he shall testify of me" (John 15:26, KJV).

The church is the bride of Christ, not the Holy Spirit. In this relationship with the church as the bride of Christ, the unfaithfulness of the church may break the bond in the relationship, but it does not hinder the Lord's great love.

The union between Christ and the church is not imaginary, but real; and as in marriage, the bride's receiving the name of the bridegroom proves the realness of the relationship. This is why the Lord's church carries the name "Christian."

Christ, the Bridegroom, has some rivals for His bride, the church. These rivals are seeking to win the love of the bride. Some of these rivals are sin, the world, and the flesh.

In this marriage of Christ and the church, the Lord's love is the cause of the marriage and the church's love is the result. The church's love is a reflected love. The apostle John said, "We love him, because he first loved us" (1 John 4:19, KJV). The Lord's love was so boundless and intense that it drew the church to Himself.

VI. The Church as the Building of Christ

A building implies a construction of progressive stages. The stages begin under the ground and proceed upward until the building is completed.

A. *The Foundation*

"For other foundation can no man lay than that is laid, which is Jesus Christ" (1 Corinthians 3:11, KJV).

Because of the value of the foundation it is worthy of further discussion. Each stage of the building is based upon that which lies below, and that is the foundation. The foundation is the most important part of any building. If the foundation is defective, all of the cost and labor of the building is in vain. A solid foundation helps to guarantee the stability and continuance of the building.

The life of a foundation lies in its strength. Christ is the foundation of the Christian church. This means that Christ is the source of the church's being. Just as there would be no building without a foundation, there would be no church without Christ.

The foundation is that from which everything springs, while at the same time it bears the weight of the building. From Christ the church gets her beauty, and all of the weight of the church is upon Him.

B. *The Cornerstone*

"Wherefore also it is contained in the scripture, Behold, I lay in Sion a chief corner stone, elect, precious: and he that believeth on him shall not be confounded" (1 Peter 2:6, KJV).

The cornerstone is one stone that stays with the building. The cornerstone supports the building, unites it, and beautifies it. The difference between laying a cornerstone in modern times and laying a cornerstone in biblical times is that whereas now the cornerstone is laid last while in biblical times it was laid first.

Today, the cornerstone of a building is merely a ceremonial cornerstone designed to contain a few records, giving the date and other information concerning the building. But in biblical times the cornerstone was placed in a building to mark the starting point in the building. This means that whatever is built should start with Jesus.

With Jesus as the cornerstone it suggests that He is valuable and chosen by God. As Christ came on the scene there were attempts on the part of the Jews to reject Him. But Peter said concerning Jesus, "This is the stone which was set at nought of you builders, which is become the head of the corner. Neither is there salvation in any other: for there is none other name under heaven given among men, whereby we must be saved" (Acts 4:11-12, KJV).

C. *The Stones in the Building*

"Ye also, as lively stones, are built up a spiritual house, an holy priesthood, to offer up spiritual sacrifices, acceptable to God by Jesus Christ" (1 Peter 2:5, KJV).

There are great buildings which men have built, but there are none which supersede the church. The church has God as its Owner. As the Owner, He has unlimited wisdom and power in the construction of the building.

The church is constructed of redeemed and regenerated people—living stones—people who have been renewed by the Holy Spirit. The stones once had no connection with the building. They were deeply imbedded in nature's rock quarry of guilt; but by the hammer of God's Word and the working of the Holy Spirit, the stones have been fitted for God's building, which is the church.

The church is not the building it is because of the perfection of the stones, but because of the artful work of the Builder and the stability of the Foundation.

It has been said that the church is a divine institution. It is divine because a divine Architect planned it; a divine Builder built it; and a divine Purchaser bought it.

Notice again the words of the background Scripture: "Upon this rock I will build my church; and the gates of hell shall not prevail against it." This passage suggests four things:

1. **Proclamation**—"Upon this rock I will build."
2. **Proprietorship**—"My church."
3. **Persecution and Death**—"The gates of hell."
4. **Preservation**—"Shall not prevail against it."

FOR DISCUSSION

1. What is a church?
2. What is the work of the church?
3. What is the stability of the church?
4. What figures are used in the Bible to describe the church?

Chapter 12

WHAT WE BELIEVE ABOUT THE ORDINANCES OF THE CHURCH
(Matthew 28:19; 1 Corinthians 11:23-26)

One issue of church life that seems valueless and unimportant is what is believed about the ordinances of the church. An *ordinance* is a rite or ceremony. It is a custom or practice that exists because of authority. The ordinances of the church should only be those which are commanded by Christ.

There are those churches and religious groups that have misunderstood the Bible's teachings on the ordinances of the church. The Bible teaches that there are two ordinances left by Jesus for the church to practice. They are baptism and the Lord's Supper.

However, there are those who practice foot washing as an ordinance of the church. This discussion is not an attempt to say that to wash feet in the church is wrong; but it is wrong to practice washing feet as a commanded ordinance from Jesus.

In this passage from John 13, Jesus was preparing to eat the Last Supper with His disciples. Before eating, Jesus got up from the table, wrapped a towel around His waist, poured water into a basin, and began washing the feet of the disciples. Peter showed some resistance to the actions of Jesus because he did not fully understand Jesus.

The washing of the feet of the disciples gave Jesus a chance to convey a spiritual truth to them. Peter told Jesus to give him a complete bath rather than just to wash his feet. But Jesus replied that those who are already clean have no need of washing, except for the feet.

Jesus said, "He who has bathed needs only to wash his feet, but is completely clean; and you are clean, but not all of you" (John 13:10). Jesus made this statement because He knew that Judas was going to betray Him (see John 13:11).

Once Jesus had finished washing the feet of the disciples, He took His place back at the head of the table and said to the disciples, "Do you know what I have done to you? You call Me Teacher and Lord; and you are right, for so I am. If I then, the Lord and the Teacher, washed your feet, you also ought to wash one another's feet. For I gave you an example that you also should do as I did to you" (John 13:12-15).

This entire incident is a lesson on love and humility being taught the disciples by Jesus. Jesus did for the disciples, in washing their feet, what a slave would have done for guests who would arrive in the slave owner's home. There was always someone available in the household to wash the dust from the feet of those who entered the house.

Nowhere in this narrative does Jesus say that the washing of feet is a command to be kept by the church. But He does say that He was setting an example for His disciples to follow in living lives of love and humility. The major concern of Jesus was not that feet were washed, but that the disciples would love and be humble in their actions and attitude.

I. The Lord's Supper

Many people have been taking the Lord's Supper for many years, yet they have not given much thought to what they believe about the Lord's Supper. For many people the Lord's Supper is just something they habitually do each first Sunday in the month. However, it does not hold any significance for them.

There are many views concerning what takes place during the time the Lord's Supper is being administered. The Catholics believe that the bread and the wine become the actual body and blood of Jesus. The Lutherans believe that the body and blood of Jesus are present in the fruit of the vine and the bread.

Then there are those who believe that by taking the Lord's Supper one receives grace through the bread and the fruit of the vine. But Baptists teach and believe that the Lord's Supper is a symbol of the suffering and death of Jesus. The bread symbolizes the broken body of Jesus, and the fruit of the vine is a symbol of His shed blood.

A. *The Lord's Supper Is a Proclamation*

"As often as you eat this bread and drink the cup, you proclaim the Lord's death" (1 Corinthians 11:26).

The Lord's Supper is the symbolic proclamation of the Gospel that is proclaimed through the preaching of the Word of God. The preaching of the Gospel is the spoken Word about the suffering and death of Jesus. The Lord's Supper is the symbol of the suffering and death of Jesus. The only difference between the two is the method.

The Lord's Supper gives every believer the opportunity to give testimony to the fact that Jesus suffered and died for all who believe. Since the Lord's Supper is the proclamation of the suffering and death of Jesus, it is therefore the proclamation of God's love for the world.

In the Lord's Supper there is the proclamation that sin has been atoned for and those who trust Jesus as Savior and Lord have been given eternal life. This eternal life cost Jesus pain and agony, and this pain and agony is symbolized in the bread and the fruit of the vine in the Lord's Supper.

B. *The Lord's Supper Is a Memorial*

Jesus said, "Do this in remembrance of Me" (1 Corinthians 11:24b-25).

It was the intent of Jesus that what He did at Golgotha would never be forgotten. Jesus was well aware of the fact that human nature soon forgets spiritual things. He also knew that there would be those who would not read their Bibles. He therefore gave the Lord's Supper as a standing provision against humanity's forgetfulness.

With the Lord's Supper as a constant reminder of the suffering and death of Jesus, believers are able to keep in closer communion with Jesus Christ, the Savior of the world. Jesus knew that a person's memory would not stay healthy by merely feeding on promises or words. He gave the Lord's Supper as a visible symbol to feed people's memories concerning the death of Jesus for man's sins. The Lord's Supper tends to increase love of the Savior to whose memory it is dedicated.

When the church shares in the Lord's Supper she expresses her gratitude to God for deliverance from sin and restored fellowship with God through Jesus Christ.

C. *The Lord's Supper Is a Prophecy*

Paul told the Corinthians, "For as often as you eat this bread and drink the cup, you proclaim the Lord's death until He comes" (1 Corinthians 11:26).

The Lord's Supper is a prophecy of the fact that the Lord's death is effective until He returns. One songwriter said that "it will never lose its power."

The Lord's Supper is a prophecy of the endurance of the church. Jesus had already said, "Upon this rock I will build My church; and the gates of Hades will not overpower it" (Matthew 16:18).

The Lord's Supper is a prophecy of the certainty of the second coming of Jesus. When the church partakes of the Lord's Supper she symbolizes the partaking of the benefits of the suffering and death of Jesus until He returns.

II. **Baptism**

A. *The Baptism of John the Baptist*

When John the Baptist came on the scene, he came "preaching a baptism of repentance for the forgiveness of sins" (Mark 1:4). When John began baptizing it was not something new to the Jews. They had been practicing baptism since the Babylonian captivity.

To the Jews, baptism meant a washing or cleansing from sins. It denoted putting away impurity for the purpose of being pure in heart and life.

The Jews made it a point and custom to baptize all Gentiles who were received into Judaism because it signified that the Gentiles had renounced paganism and had taken on a new form of religion.

But John the Baptist gave baptism a new purpose. It signified the washing away of those sins of which the person had repented. It was a baptism that dealt with man's actions in regards to sin.

However, when Jesus came to John to be baptized, He had no sin of which to repent. Jesus submitted to baptism in order to give it an even greater purpose than that which John had given it. When Jesus spoke to John concerning his baptizing Him, John tried to prevent the baptism of Jesus by saying that he had a need to be baptized by Jesus. But Jesus said, "Permit it at this time; for in this way it is fitting for us to fulfill all righteousness" (Matthew 3:15).

The baptism of Jesus made baptism a divine ordinance. It gave a divine stamp of approval on the ministry of John the Baptist. The baptism of Jesus was also a formal identification of Jesus as Messiah.

B. *The Candidates for Baptism*

There are some religious groups that baptize babies. But the Bible does not teach this practice.

As Jesus gave His disciples the Great Commission in Mark 16:15-16, He said, "Go into all the world and preach the gospel to all creation. He who has believed and has been baptized shall be saved."

This passage does not suggest that water baptism is essential to salvation. Baptism is the outward profession of the change that has taken place as a result of believing. It is also the door into the church.

A baby is not a proper candidate for baptism because a baby is incapable of believing in Jesus as Savior and Lord.

In Baptist churches, many pastors baptize persons who come from other denominations. There are those who feel that pastors are in error for doing this because the Bible says, "One Lord, one faith, one baptism" (Ephesians 4:5).

Reading verses 3-5 from this passage in Ephesians 4 reveals that Paul was dealing with the unifying work of the Holy Spirit. For that reason, "one baptism" seems to have reference to one baptism of the Holy Spirit.

Proper baptism requires three things; a proper candidate, which is a saved person; a proper mode, which is immersion; and a proper administrator, which is a Baptist preacher.

C. *The Mode of Baptism*

There are certain religious groups that teach that there are three modes of baptism—immersion, pouring, and sprinkling. The reason they teach pouring and sprinkling as modes of baptism is because of a mistranslation of the Greek word *baptizo*. This word means "to dip under; to sink; to immerse; to drown."

Where the word *baptizo* is found in the Greek text some translators used the word *rhantizo*. This word has reference to the act of spraying or sprinkling on something or with something.

A look at Jesus' being baptized of John reveals that He came up out of the water. When Philip baptized the Ethiopian eunuch, both of them came up out of the water. There is nowhere in the Bible where sprinkling or pouring of water was used as a mode of baptism. Any person who has not been immersed is still a candidate for baptism.

D. *The Meaning of Baptism*

Baptism is the symbol of the death, burial, and resurrection of Jesus. Through baptism, the church symbolizes her being crucified with Christ. Paul said, "Do you not know that all of us who have been baptized into Christ Jesus have been baptized into his death?" (Romans 6:3). Baptism is a testimony that a person has died to sin; he or she has experienced a change in his or her nature.

Whenever anyone dies, the next thing is to plan that person's burial. Once a person has died to sin, baptism symbolizes being buried.

Paul said, "Therefore we have been buried with Him through baptism into death, so that as Christ was raised from the dead through the glory of the Father, so we too might walk in newness of life. For if we have become united with Him in the likeness of His death, certainly we shall also be in the likeness of His resurrection" (Romans 6:4-5).

When a person is buried he or she is supposed to be out of sight and on his or her way to not being recognized anymore. In baptism, the candidate symbolizes the old man's being put to death and buried, and the resurrection of a new man who walks with Jesus.

Paul said to the Corinthians, "If anyone is in Christ, he is a new creature; the old things passed away; behold, new things have come" (2 Corinthians 5:17).

FOR DISCUSSION

1. What are the ordinances of the church commanded by Jesus?
2. Why did Jesus leave these ordinances for the church to keep?
3. Why did Jesus submit to baptism?
4. Who are the candidates for baptism?
5. What is the meaning of the Lord's Supper?
6. Who should take the Lord's Supper?

Chapter 13

WHAT WE BELIEVE ABOUT THE CORRECT DAY OF WORSHIP
(Exodus 20:8; Revelation 1:10)

One area of discussion that creates much concern and wonder is identifying the correct day that the Lord appointed for the church to worship. There are those religious groups that believe the seventh day, the Sabbath, is the correct day of worship. This is so because of the misunderstanding of the Sabbath that was kept by the children of Israel in the Old Testament and the Jewish nation in the New Testament.

Study of the correct day for the church to worship is seldom addressed through preaching or teaching in the Baptist church.

The word *Sabbath* means "rest." It was a day of physical rest for the Jews and there was no work to be done by anyone, even the servants of the household. It seemed in New Testament times that those who were keepers of the Sabbath were not even permitted to perform deeds of kindness on the Sabbath, which Jesus challenged with an example of a situation of life and death in Matthew 12:8-14).

I. God's Reason for Giving the Sabbath to Israel

When Moses was given the Ten Commandments on Mount Sinai, the fourth commandment was "Remember the sabbath day, to keep it holy" (Exodus 20:8). The Sabbath followed six days of labor and would be our present day of Saturday.

It is important to understand that the only persons who were ever required to keep the Sabbath were the Jews. This was so because it was a sign of their being chosen by God as His representatives.

God said to Ezekiel while Israel was in Babylonian captivity, "I gave them My sabbaths to be a sign between Me and them, that they might know that I am the LORD who sanctifies them" (Ezekiel 20:12). The idea of the Sabbath as being a sign between God and Israel is also taught in Exodus 31:13, 16-17.

A sign is something that does not call attention to itself for the sake of itself. A sign directs the onlooker to something greater than itself. A sign teaches and gives guidance. The Sabbath was a sign of the covenant between God and Israel just like circumcision was, but neither the Sabbath nor circumcision was commanded to be kept by the Gentiles.

Paul said to the Colossians, "No one is to act as your judge in regard to food or drink or in respect to a festival or a new moon or a Sabbath day—things which are a mere shadow of what is to come; but the substance belongs to Christ" (Colossians 2:16-17).

Jesus said concerning the Sabbath, "For the Son of Man is Lord of the Sabbath" (Matthew 12:8).

When Jesus was passing through the grain fields on the Sabbath and His disciples began picking grain, the Pharisees began saying that the disciples were doing something unlawful. But Jesus said, "The Sabbath was made for man, and not man for the Sabbath. So the Son of Man is Lord even of the Sabbath" (Mark 2:27-28).

II. Sunday as a Monument of the Resurrection of Jesus

In Matthew 28:1, Mary Magdalene and the other Mary came to the tomb of Jesus after the Sabbath, as it began to dawn toward the first day of the week. Upon their arrival, they discovered that Jesus had risen from the grave, just as He said He would.

God's plan of salvation hinges upon the resurrection of Jesus. The apostle Paul said that if Jesus is not risen from the dead, then faith is vain, preaching is vain, Christians are false witnesses, they are still in their sins, and there is no resurrection of the dead (see 1 Corinthians 15:12-18). As a monument to remember the resurrection of Jesus, the early church worshipped on the first day of the week and not on the seventh day.

There were numerous occasions when both Jesus and Paul met with Jews in their synagogues and preached to them. But they were doing what any wise man would do: they were going where they knew they would get an audience. However, the New Testament church's coming together for worship was always on Sunday, the first day of the week.

Jesus was resurrected from the grave on the first day of the week. His first appearance to the disciples was on the first day of the week. The second appearance of Jesus to His disciples was on the first day of the week.

Not only is the first day of the week a monument to the resurrection of Jesus, but it is also a monument of the coming of the Holy Spirit upon the church for the purpose of empowering her for works of service. The Day of Pentecost came fifty days after the resurrection of Jesus, and that was the first day of the week, which is Sunday.

On several occasions, the New Testament records the fact that the first day of the week held special significance for the early church. Paul said to the Corinthians, "On the first day of every week is to each one of you is to put aside and save, as he may prosper, so that no collections be made when I come" (1 Corinthians 16:2).

For the apostle Paul to make this plea, the church had to have some habit, practice, or routine of meeting on the first day of the week.

When the apostle Paul sailed from Philippi and went to Troas, Luke the historian said, "On the first day of the week, when we were gathered together to break bread, Paul began talking to them, intending to leave the next day, and he prolonged his message until midnight" (Acts 20:7).

Here again is the New Testament church meeting together on the first day of the week.

When the apostle John was banished to the Isle of Patmos, he was isolated for the Word of the Lord. But in spite of his isolation he was insulated. John said, "I was in the Spirit on the Lord's day" (Revelation 1:10a).

It was on the Lord's Day that Jesus gave him his commission to become a writer. Jesus said to John on the Lord's Day, "Write in a book what you see, and send it to the seven churches: to Ephesus and to Smyrna and to Pergamum and to Thyatira and to Sardis and to Philadelphia and to Laodicea" (Revelation 1:11).

It was also on the Lord's Day that Jesus revealed Himself to John like John had never seen Him before. John said the following: "I turned to see the voice that was speaking with me. And having turned I saw seven golden lampstands; and in the middle of the lampstands I saw one like a son of man, clothed in a robe reaching to the feet, and girded across His chest with a golden sash. His head and His hair were white like white wool, like snow; and His eyes were like a flame of fire. His feet were like burnished bronze, when it has been made to glow in a furnace, and His voice was like the sound of many waters. In His right hand He held seven stars, and out of His mouth came a sharp two-edged sword; and His face was like the sun shining in its strength." (Revelation 1:12-16)

Just what was it that Jesus was revealing to John on the Lord's Day? Consider these eight revelations:

A. *The Robe Reaching to the Feet*—the Kingship of Jesus

B. *The White Hair*—the Wisdom and Holiness of Jesus

C. *The Eyes like a Flaming Fire*—the Omniscience or All-knowingness of Jesus

D. *The Feet like Burnished Bronze*—the Power of Jesus to Crush Evil

E. *The Voice of Many Waters*—the Authority of Jesus

F. *The Seven Stars in the Right Hand*—the Pastors of the Churches

G. *The Sharp, Two-edged Sword*—the Power of the Word of God to Protect the Church

H. *The Face Shining as the Sun* — the Greatness and Majesty of Jesus

John saw all of this in Jesus while in the Spirit on the Lord's Day.

▶ FOR DISCUSSION

1. What was the significance of the Sabbath?

2. What part does the Sabbath play in the life of the New Testament church?

3. Why does the New Testament church worship on Sunday?

Chapter 14

WHAT WE BELIEVE ABOUT THE CHURCH AND ITS MISSION
(Matthew 28:18-20)

When Jesus organized the church He had a purpose and a plan for her. He organized the church to fight the evil forces in the world and to be His witnesses.

The church is not a building; the building is the place where the church meets. The church is in the hearts of believing men, women, boys, and girls.

The church has a mission. The word *mission* means "to go or send." No believer was excluded from this mission. The church's mission is the same as that of Jesus; to preach, teach, and heal (see Matthew 4:23). This mission has not changed. All throughout the Bible God can be seen as a sending God.

There are some places where some individuals cannot go. There are some things some persons cannot do. Then it becomes their mission to go where they can, give to those who can go where they cannot, and pray for those on the missionary field.

The missionary church is the church that is not solely concerned with herself. It is a church for others. The missionary church is the church that makes the salvation of the world a priority.

The missionary church is in the world but not of the world. The effectiveness of the church is dependent upon the church's making contact with the world; yet, the church must not allow itself to conform to the world. There is at least one caution for the church, and that is the possibility of spiritual pride.

I. Missions Is an Obligation and not an Option

The continuation of the church is based on the continuation of God's mission into which the church has been called. Missions is nothing more than believers following God's design for His church.

Jesus said to His disciples in the Sermon on the Mount, "You are the salt of the earth"; "You are the light of the world" (Matthew 5:13, 14).

This is not to say what the church is to become, but rather what the church is. If the world is to be preserved from ruin it will be because the church fulfills her purpose of being salt. Salt is only effective when it makes contact with that which would otherwise decay.

If the world is to be brought out of the darkness of sin, it will be because the church fulfills her purpose of being light. Light is only helpful when it can be seen.

The fulfilling of the church's mission is the result of her dedication to the will of God. Too many people put forth special effort to avoid the will of God. But the church is here to build and rebuild itself through missions.

The fulfilling of the church's mission is also to be understood as dependence upon the Holy Spirit. The Holy Spirit guides the church in her work of missions. The Holy Spirit empowers the church in her work of missions; and the Holy Spirit regenerates the soul of the believer.

The Spirit-filled church is always the church that is fulfilling the mission given by Jesus Christ. The Spirit-filled church is aware that missions is an obligation and not an option.

II. Missions Is an Evidence of God's Concern for the World

In John 3:16, Jesus said, "For God so loved the world, that He gave His only begotten Son, that whoever believes in Him shall not perish, but have eternal life."

Jesus said to Zacchaeus, "For the Son of Man has come to seek and to save that which was lost" (Luke 19:10).

The apostle Paul said to the Corinthians, "For you know the grace of our Lord Jesus Christ, that though He was rich, yet for your sake He became poor, so that you through His poverty might become rich" (2 Corinthians 8:9).

Jesus Christ came into the world as an expression of God's love for the world. It did not matter to Him that the world was sinful. In fact, if there had been no sinners in the world there would have been no reason for Jesus to come.

Now, what the church needs to understand is that just as Jesus was God in the flesh, she is Jesus in the flesh. Therefore, the church's reason for being here should be the same as Jesus' reason for coming into the world. No, the church cannot save the lost as Jesus did, but the church can seek them.

Seeing a sinner on his or her way to hell ought to be a heartbreaking experience for a Christian.

God has a healthy love for Himself, and any time a sinner goes to hell that is a part of the likeness and image of God going there. This is why the missionary task is so valuable. God expects the church to love the same world He loves. He also expects the church to seek the salvation of the same world He came to save.

The circumstances or conditions for doing what the Lord said to do are not always favorable. When world conditions are considered during the time when Jesus came into the world they were not favorable. In fact, if Jesus had come into the world when conditions were favorable for His reception, He would have never come.

The church cannot wait until everybody gives a "yes" vote to missions. The church must start where she is, use what she has, and make the best out of it.

When the church is engaged in missions she gives a testimony of God's concern for the world.

III. Missions Assures the Power and Presence of Jesus for the Church

Jesus said to His disciples on Resurrection morning, "All power is given unto me in heaven and in earth. Go ye therefore, and teach all nations, baptizing them in the name of the Father, and of the Son, and of the Holy Ghost: Teaching them to observe all things whatsoever I have commanded you: and, lo, I am with you always, even unto the end of the world" (Matthew 28:18-20, KJV).

If there is no spiritual power then the church is as helpless in the world as a dead body.

But Jesus gives the church sufficient power to be His witnesses in the world.

There are two major reasons for why Jesus offers His power and presence: to evangelize and to Christianize.

The parting message Jesus spoke to His disciples was, "You will receive power when the Holy Spirit has come upon you; and you shall be My witnesses both in Jerusalem, and in all Judea and Samaria, and even to the remotest part of the earth" (Acts 1:8).

When the church is busy doing the work that God has designed for her to do, she has the assurance of the power and presence of Jesus.

> Jesus is before the church to be her guide.
> Jesus is behind the church to be her protector.
> Jesus is beside the church to be her comforter.
> Jesus is around the church to be her companion.
> Jesus is within the church to be her source of power.
> Jesus is beneath the church to be her sure foundation.

▶ FOR DISCUSSION

1. How can one recognize a Spirit-filled church?

2. How does God presently show His love for the world?

3. How can the church be assured of the power and presence of the Holy Spirit?

Chapter 15

WHAT WE BELIEVE ABOUT THE WORK OF THE HOLY SPIRIT IN THE LIFE OF THE CHURCH
(Luke 4:16-19; Acts 1:8)

In the year of AD 29, Jesus stood at Caesarea Philippi and said, "Upon this rock I will build My church" (Matthew 16:18). This is the origin of the New Testament church. In the second chapter of the book of Acts, the church that was founded by Jesus was empowered by the Holy Spirit.

The Holy Spirit did for the church what He did for all creation: He gave it life and order. Because of the Holy Spirit the church is more than an organization; it is an organism which should have organization.

In this background Scripture from Luke 4:16-19, Jesus had recently left the wilderness of temptation, after being led there by the Holy Spirit to be tempted by the devil. Luke said, "And Jesus returned to Galilee in the power of the Spirit" (Luke 4:14a).

Some time after His arrival in Galilee, Jesus decided to visit His hometown of Nazareth. In Nazareth, He went into the synagogue and stood up and read publicly an Old Testament passage of Scripture concerning His call to preach.

Jesus read from Isaiah 61:1-2a, "THE SPIRIT OF THE LORD IS UPON ME, BECAUSE HE ANOINTED ME TO PREACH THE GOSPEL TO THE POOR. HE HAS SENT ME TO PROCLAIM RELEASE TO THE CAPTIVES, AND RECOVERY OF SIGHT TO THE BLIND, TO SET FREE THOSE WHO ARE OPPRESSED, TO PROCLAIM THE FAVORABLE YEAR OF THE LORD" (Luke 4:18-19).

In this passage, Jesus proclaimed Himself to be the Anointed One, the Messiah. He also proclaimed the direction that His ministry would take. The ministry of the Anointed One was to be a ministry of seeking the salvation of humankind.

It is worth noting how Jesus showed the salvation of humankind; He showed it as healing from broken-heartedness, deliverance from captivity, recovering of sight, and freedom from oppression. The ministry of Jesus was one of spiritual healing and spiritual freedom. The preparation for this ministry was by the anointing of the Holy Spirit.

Since the New Testament church is the incarnation of Jesus, and since she has been given the task of continuing the work that was begun by Jesus, she also needs the anointing of the Holy Spirit.

This lesson shall focus on the work of the Holy Spirit in the life of the church. Once this lesson is concluded there will be more that could be said than there has been said.

I. The Holy Spirit Works the Work of Salvation

Jesus said to Nicodemus, "That which is born of the flesh is flesh, and that which is born of the Spirit is spirit" (John 3:6).

In this passage the words that are usually given emphasis are the words *born, flesh,* and *spirit.* But another important word is the little preposition *of.* This word suggests the direction of the birth. It suggests something coming out from something else, as a baby coming out of the womb of its mother.

The Holy Spirit causes the soul to experience a delivery of a person's nature which totally revolutionizes that person's life, just like a baby coming forth from its mother's womb.

II. The Holy Spirit Makes the Gospel Intelligible

On the Day of Pentecost, when the Holy Spirit descended upon the church, there were persons of various nationalities in Jerusalem at that time. When the Holy Spirit descended upon the church, the members of the church began to witness for Christ in the languages of those who were present.

The members of the church were not speaking some mystical, magical, or unknown language. They were speaking the languages of the people present. Those who were there said to one another,

"Are not all these who are speaking Galileans? And how is it that we each hear them in our own language to which we were born?" (Acts 2:7-8).

The answer to their questions lay in the work of the Holy Spirit. He made the Gospel that was preached by the disciples intelligible to all who were present.

There can be no salvation or Christian growth unless the Word of God is understood by those who hear it.

If the Holy Spirit inspired the Bible, then it also takes the Holy Spirit to understand it.

III. The Holy Spirit Produces Unity in the Church

After the Holy Spirit descended upon the church at Jerusalem on the Day of Pentecost, He produced unity among people, unity of practice, and unity in prayer in the church. "They were continually devoting themselves to the apostles' teaching and to fellowship" (Acts 2:42).

The Holy Spirit also produced unity of possessions in the church in Jerusalem. "All those who had believed were together and had all things in common . . . and were sharing . . . with all, as anyone might have need" (Acts 2:44, 45).

The church at Jerusalem had unity in their praise of God on the Day of Pentecost, for they worshipped together regularly. "Day by day continuing with one mind in the temple . . . praising God, and having favor with all the people. And the Lord was adding to their number day by day those who were being saved" (Acts 2:46, 47).

IV. The Holy Spirit Secures the Salvation of the Church (Ephesians 1:13-14)

Paul said to the Ephesians, "In Him (Jesus Christ), you also, after listening to the message of truth . . . having also believed, you were sealed in Him with the Holy Spirit of promise, who is given as a pledge of our inheritance, with a view to the redemption of God's own possession, to the praise of His glory."

God purchased the church by the blood of Christ; now He is taking over what belongs to Him by the work of the Holy Spirit.

The Holy Spirit is God's seal, pledging that the saved shall be finally and completely delivered from the power and presence of sin.

Paul said to the Romans, "But if the Spirit of Him who raised Jesus from the dead dwells in you, He who raised Christ Jesus from the dead will also give life to your mortal bodies through His Spirit who dwells in you" (Romans 8:11).

The Holy Spirit guarantees the salvation of the soul and also the body.

V. The Holy Spirit Empowers the Church to Be Witnesses (Acts 1:8)

Jesus said, "You will receive power when the Holy Spirit has come upon you; and you shall be My witnesses both in Jerusalem, and in all Judea and Samaria, and even to the remotest part of the earth."

The two key ideas in this passage center in what the church shall receive and what the church shall be. "You shall receive power . . . You shall be My witnesses."

The real business of the church is not just to witness for Christ in the world. The church is to be witnesses. This means that because of the work of the Holy Spirit, witnessing becomes a lifestyle of the church and not just an activity in the church.

▶ **FOR DISCUSSION**

1. Why is the church an organism rather than just an organization?

2. What was the preparatory factor in the ministry of Jesus?

3. What does the Holy Spirit do for the church in relationship to the Gospel?

4. What part does the Holy Spirit play in the act of soul winning?

▶ BIOGRAPHY ◀

REVEREND GEORGE T. BROOKS SR. received a B.A. degree from the American Baptist College and was an outstanding honor student and a Master of Divinity from Faith Evangelical Seminary in Tacoma, Washington. He received a Doctor of Divinity degree from the Shiloh Theological Seminary in Stafford, Virginia.

He is married to Sarah Brooks and has a daughter, Octavia, and son, the Reverend George T. Brooks Jr. He is the grandfather of five.

Reverend Brooks pastored Friendship Baptist Church in Cross Plains, Tennessee, and is presently pastor of Saint James Missionary Baptist Church, where he has served since June of 1984. He also served as the director of Pastoral Studies Field Work and Practical Christian Service at American Baptist College for three years.

He has been very active in other religious and civic activities. He is a former commissioner of the Historical Commission and the Human Relation Commissions of Metropolitan Nashville Davidson County. He is a member of 100 Black Men of Middle Tennessee. He served two years as second vice moderator of the Little Fork District Association, seven years as president of the Congress of the Missionary Baptist State Convention of Tennessee, two years as deputy secretary of the Christian Education Board of the National Baptist Convention of America, Incorporated, and two years as the chairman of that same board. He served as the second vice moderator of the Nashville City Missionary Baptist District Association for eight years.

Reverend Brooks was elected president of the Missionary Baptist State Convention of Tennessee in October 1995, which gave him leadership to some 130 churches in the Middle Tennessee Area. He served until July 2003. He was appointed director of the Congress of Christian Workers of the National Baptist Convention of America, Inc. in September 2003 and served until September 2009. He was then appointed fourth vice president.

Out of his concern for the community, he and the church gave two lots to Habitat for Humanity, which house non-church members. This venture created an interest at heart that led him to a joint venture between the church and the private sector to develop and build fifty-two affordable houses.

He has received numerous awards and has written eleven books: *Fruits of Fellowship; Believing as Baptists; Praising and Worshiping God; The Pastor's Love Offering; Saved, Satisfied and Secure; Offering God My Substance and Myself; Great Sermons from Our Past; The Covenant We Practice; The Letter to the Colossians; From the Heart of the President;* and *God's Use Of A Man Called Nehemiah.* He also has a total of twenty-six (26) books that are now available on Wordsearch, one of the most comprehensive computer Bible programs available today. This includes the books listed above.

By the leading of the Holy Spirit, his consistent challenge to the church is to strive to become "A Church to Match This Hour."

www.ingramcontent.com/pod-product-compliance
Lightning Source LLC
Chambersburg PA
CBHW071537080526
44588CB00011B/1696